ADMIRAL BYRD'S SECRET JOURNEY BEYOND THE POLES

Global Communications/Conspiracy Journal

ADMIRAL BYRD'S SECRET JOURNEY BEYOND THE POLES

Tim R. Swartz

ISBN-10: 0938294989
ISBN-13: 978-0938294986

Nonfiction – Metaphysics

Timothy Green Beckley: Editorial Director
Carol Rodriguez: Publishers Assistant
Cover Art: Tim Swartz

1. Swartz, Tim, Bible, Metaphysics – Nonfiction
I. Title: Admiral Byrd's Secret Journey Beyond The Poles

133'.0

For free catalog write:
Global Communications
P.O. Box 753
New Brunswick, NJ 08903

www.conspiracyjournal.com

 CONTENTS

Admiral Byrd's Secret Journey Beyond the Poles

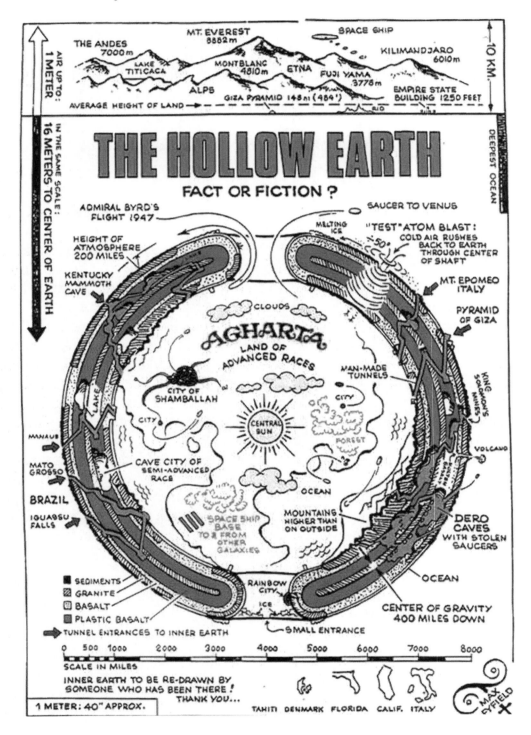

Admiral Byrd's Secret Journey Beyond the Poles

<u>Forward</u>

We like to think that we know so much about the world that we live in. We enjoy knowing things like why the sky is blue and why the grass is green. With knowledge comes power and security. We feel secure knowing things that at one time confounded our forbearers.

We are secure in our knowledge that our solar system is part of the Milky Way galaxy, one of billions of other galaxies in the universe. We are secure in our knowledge that the sun is in the center of the solar system and that the Earth, along with the other planets, circles the sun. We are secure in our knowledge that the Earth is round and turns on its axis as makes its way around the sun.

We like to think that we know so much about the world that we live in. But, in all actuality, there is so much that we just do not know. We loathe this lack of knowledge; it makes us feel frightened and insecure. It makes us feel like how early man must have felt when he stood on the African plains and trembled in fear at the crack of lightning accompanied by the ear-splitting roar of thunder. We feel tiny and insignificant.

Because of these feelings, when humans lack real knowledge about something we have a tendency to simply make things up in an attempt to fill that intellectual gap. When we didn't know the science behind lightning and thunder, we created a pantheon of gods whose anger became material in the form of bolts of fire from the heavens. When we didn't know what was beyond the earth and sky, we envisioned a giant turtle that held the world steadfast upon its immense back.

When it became clear that there was no turtle holding the universe in place, philosophers placed the Earth at the center of creation with everything in the heavens revolving around it in an eternal dance of celestial obedience. This, however, did not sit well with those who still believed in the turtle. After all, the Earth as a round ball drifting in empty space seemed totally illogical; how could the Earth float magically without something to hold it in place. Where were the facts? Where was the proof? Where was the turtle?

Those who believed that the Earth was the center of the universe made fun of the turtle believers. How could anyone believe in anything as stupid as a giant turtle holding the planet on its back? It was abundantly clear that God created the Earth so that means the Earth was the center of every thing. Sorry, no room in God's universe for a big turtle.

However, those who believed in an Earth-centric universe did not have long to bask in their glory. A new kid on the block by the name of Copernicus told everyone that their long cherished beliefs were wrong, the Earth, along with the other planets, revolved around the sun.

Admiral Byrd's Secret Journey Beyond the Poles

This, of course, seemed pretty rude to the "Earth is the center of creation" believers. Where were the facts they asked? Where was the proof? How could God, who the Bible says made the Earth a special place, not put it in the center of everything?

For a while, those who believed in the "Copernicus Theory" were severely persecuted by those who refused to let go of their long-held beliefs. Eventually it became clear that knowledge had once more progressed, leaving the past behind and old beliefs abandoned in the dust.

Yet, things never really change. We say that we know so much, when we actually know very little. Geologists say that the Earth at its very center is composed of extremely dense, extremely hot, crystallized iron and nickel. However, there are those who say that the Earth is hollow and inside this subterranean realm there exists a world almost beyond belief; a world that is home to a rich diversity of life and, as some say, civilizations of superior beings who are the true masters of this planet.

Scientists say that this is impossible, that the Earth is solid through and through. However, at this point in time, no scientist has actually ever been far enough underground to prove their theories. On the other hand, there have been plenty of people throughout the centuries who have claimed to have journeyed to the underground world, seen the sights, met the people, and returned to tell their tales.

The ancient writings of the Chinese, Egyptians, Hindus and other races, and the legends of the Eskimos, speak of a great opening in the north and a race that lives under the earth's crust, and that their ancestors came from this paradisiacal land in the Earth's interior. Some Native American tribes have stories that tell of their ancestors who came from a sacred land from somewhere deep within the planet. The Inuit who live in the frozen wastelands of the arctic say that they originally came from a warm land of perpetual sunlight located somewhere beyond the North Pole.

The ancient Irish had a legend of a land beyond the sea where the sun always shone and it was always summer weather. They even thought that some of their heroes had gone there and returned – after which they were never satisfied with their own country.

Our knowledge of what lies beneath our feet is pretty slim. This makes a lot of people feel frightened and insecure. So they try to fill that gap in knowledge with theories and personal beliefs systems. But instead of taking the word of those who have never been beyond the first few feet of dirt in their backyard garden, perhaps we should consider those who say that they have been under the crust of the planet. Maybe we should listen to those who say that there is more to this world than we know; that there is another world underneath us that is ripe for discovery and exploration for those who are willing to take the chance and expand their knowledge.

Maybe there is even room somewhere for that big turtle.

Admiral Byrd's Secret Journey Beyond the Poles

Can it be possible that down in the middle of the Earth there is another Earth? That a few hundred miles or so away, separated from us by ground and rock and vapor and such things, there is a great country inhabited by a great race?

Admiral Byrd's Secret Journey Beyond the Poles

CHAPTER ONE
A Theory That Refuses to Die

As theories go, the idea that the Earth is hollow does not garner a lot of respect. For most people, the hollow Earth is probably a close second to the "Earth is flat" theory on that big list of "crack-pot" ideas. Nevertheless, as long as there have been people able to sit around a campfire, tales of a mysterious inner world have been part of mankind's heritage.

Unlike the flat Earth, or even the giant turtle, the hollow Earth has not disappeared into that great dustbin of quaint and old-fashioned myths of our ancestors. No longer does anyone have stories to tell of angels taking them up on high to view the flat Earth; but even into this modern age of spaceflight and personal computers, there are still claims of personal encounters with the lands and people of the inner world.

The idea of the hollow Earth is still so tantalizing that Dr. Brooks Agnew, a physicist and engineer, is planning an upcoming expedition to the inner Earth in an attempt to find the northern polar opening. Dr. Agnew hopes to board the commercially owned Russian icebreaker Yamal in the port of Murmansk, and to sail into the polar sea just beyond Canada's Arctic islands.

"Everest has been climbed a hundred times," Mr. Agnew says. "The Titanic has been scanned from stem to stern. [But] this is the first and only expedition to the North Pole opening ever attempted."

Dr. Agnew is the latest in a long line of people to suggest the theory that humans live on the surface of a hollow planet, in which two undiscovered openings, near the North and South poles, connect the outer Earth with an interior realm. In the 17th century, English astronomer and mathematician Sir Edmond Halley, who calculated the orbit of Halley's Comet, advanced hollow-Earth theories, as did German scientist Athanasius Kircher.

More recently the myth has experienced a slight revival, thanks in part to a 2006 book, by American author David Standish, titled ***Hollow Earth: The long and curious history of imagining strange lands, fantastical creatures, advanced civilizations, and marvelous machines below the Earth's surface***.

A year before the book was published; a Utah adventure guide named Steve Currey also tried to cash in on the hollow- Earth legend, by organizing an expedition to locate the North polar opening. Currey made a living organizing rafting trips to the world's wildest rivers. He knew how to hype exotic destinations and recruit would-be explorers on trips of a lifetime.

Admiral Byrd's Secret Journey Beyond the Poles

It's not clear whether Currey was a true hollow-Earth believer, or if he could simply see a good business opportunity. Whatever his beliefs, Currey somehow pinpointed the Arctic portal at 84.4 degrees north and 41 degrees east, roughly 400 kilometers northwest of Ellesmere Island. The North Pole inner Earth expedition was scheduled for the summer of 2006, with spaces offered to anyone with $20,000 to spare.

"There are no guarantees that this expedition will reach inner Earth," Currey cautioned on his Web site. "The expedition will make a good-faith effort to locate the North Polar opening and enter therein, but worst-case scenario is that we visit the geographic North Pole, explore the region, and continue on..."

When Currey died suddenly of brain cancer it was thought that the expedition would have to be cancelled, fortunately, Dr. Agnew stepped in to take his place. The trip was postponed to 2008. While he insists the journey has a genuine scientific purpose, Mr. Agnew also says the expedition will include several experts in meditation, mythology and UFOs, as well as a team of documentary filmmakers.

Randy Freeman, a Yellowknife writer commenting in the current issue of *Up Here* magazine, warns that; "besides heaps of throwaway cash, prospective cruisers should bring along enough gullibility to swallow an outlandish theory that, despite centuries of scorn, refuses to die."

However, Dr. Agnew is unfazed by such criticism, promising a grand polar adventure, no matter what the outcome. If the polar opening isn't there, the voyage "will still make an outstanding documentary," he promises. "But if we do find something, this will be the greatest geological discovery in the history of the world."

A SENSE OF ADVENTURE

What is it about the hollow Earth theory that continues to fascinate people? Perhaps it is because people love a good mystery and right now there are not a lot of good mysteries left for people to cling to. The surface of the planet has been almost completely explored, and now we are taking those first steps to penetrate the vast reaches of outer space. So what does that leave for the rest of us who have that primal urge to see what lies on the other side of the mountain?

The deepest parts of the oceans are still almost completely untouched by human exploration, but it is not so easy for most of us to do that sort of exploring. You either have to have a whole lot of money or the ability to hold your breath for a really long time to do any serious undersea exploration.

The idea that deep below the surface of the planet there lies a vast new world just ripe for discovery sends a tingle down the spine of anyone who grew up reading paperback books about lost cities and the wild things that lay hidden in the forbidding

Admiral Byrd's Secret Journey Beyond the Poles

jungle. The writer Edgar Rice Burroughs helped fuel those teenage passions for undiscovered worlds and brave explorations with his action adventure Pelucidar novels.

In Burroughs' concept, the Earth is a hollow shell with Pellucidar as the internal surface of that shell. Pellucidar is accessible to the surface world via polar openings allowing passage between the inner and outer worlds. Although the inner surface of the Earth has an absolute smaller area than the outer, Pellucidar actually has a greater land area, as its continents mirror the surface world's oceans and its oceans mirror the surface continents.

Something that was strange about Pellucidar's geography is that due to the concave curvature of its surface there is no horizon; the further distant something is, the higher it appears to be, until it is finally lost in the atmospheric haze. Anywhere you might be in Pellucidar, it looks as if you are smack in the middle of a giant bowl.

Pellucidar is lit by a miniature sun suspended at the center of the hollow sphere, so it is always overhead wherever one is in Pellucidar. The sole exception is the region directly under a tiny geostationary moon of the internal sun; that region as a result is under a perpetual eclipse and is known as the Land of Awful Shadow.

The miniature sun never changes in brightness, and never sets; so with no night or seasonal progression, the natives have little concept of time. The events of the series suggest that time is elastic, passing at different rates in different areas of Pellucidar and varying even in single locales.

The stories initially involve the adventures of mining heir David Innes and his inventor friend Abner Perry. In the first novel, *At the Earth's Core*, Innes and Perry accidentally discover the world is hollow after they use an "iron mole" to burrow 500 miles into the planet's crust. There they discover a wild land of primitive people living alongside dinosaurs and other fantastic creatures.

The land that Innes and Perry find themselves is ruled by the cities of the Mahars, intelligent flying reptiles resembling pterosaurs with psychic powers, who keep the local humans in subjugation. Innes and Perry eventually unite the tribes to overthrow the Mahars' domain and establish a human "Empire of Pellucidar" in its place.

Burroughs books were entirely fictional, but he obviously was familiar with the hollow Earth theories that were popular at the beginning of the 20th century. Burroughs logically thought through some of the peculiarities of what the hollow interior of the planet could be like; this is why the Pellucidar books, despite their standard action adventure plots, read like someone had actually been there.

Edgar Rice Burroughs certainly had access to plenty of hollow Earth related material that he could draw details for use in his novels. *At the Earth's Core* was written in 1914 and long before that, books such as Willis George Emerson's ***The Smoky God, or A Voyage to the Inner World*** had been published that helped solidify the hollow Earth mythos.

Admiral Byrd's Secret Journey Beyond the Poles

The Chicago Tribune on July 20, 1890 published an article about the early hollow Earth theorist Dr. Cyrus R. Teed. The title of the piece is: BLASPHEMY AND FOLLY - Chicago the Scene of a Pretended New Dispensation To Fools the Pleasure is as Great of Being Cheated as to Cheat – The Very Ideal of a Charlatan – Impudent Absurdity – New Cosmogony – New Heavens, Earth, Lies, and Victims – The Press the Enemy of All Good – Ranting Nauseating Rather than Ridiculous.

Obviously the editors took a dim view of Tweed and his wild ideas, one being that he was the Son of God. Tweed also explained to the reporter his hollow Earth beliefs.

One of Dr. Teed's revelations was to the effect that this "world is hollow," though he did not wind up his announcement in the stereotyped fashion by saying that his doll is stuffed with sawdust. O, dear, no! Dr. Teed is nothing if not original. He said "the world is hollow and we live on the inside of it instead of the outside as the astronomers suppose.

This is the way he disposes of the worthless theories of astronomers.

"The hollow sphere in which we live is about 8,000 miles in diameter with the sun at the center. A vertical line drawn from any point on this surface through the sun would strike the other side of the earth."

"This rather upsets the center of gravity," remarked an irreverent newspaper man.

"And the other theory if true would upset you," remarked Cyrus conclusively. "The fact upon which the argument of the earth's rotund convexity is founded instead of proving its convexity proves its concavity, as the Koreshan argument easily establishes. If the earth's inhabitable surface is convex man always stands vertical, the foot of the perpendicular axis of his body being directed toward the center of the earth, provided the center of the earth is the center of gravity."

"Why does the top of a ship's mast appear first on the approach of a vessel at sea?"

If the reporter thought the doctor would be stumped for an answer and have to resort to the one given in the Elementary Geography he was mistaken.

The Chicago Tribune was highly skeptical of Dr. Tweed and his theories. A short article five years later in the March 31, 1895 edition of the *Tribune* stated: "The purpose of the [Dr. Tweed's] address seemed to be to prove that "the earth is a hollow sphere, the surface of which is concave, and the inhabitants live on the inside instead of the outside of this sphere."

Admiral Byrd's Secret Journey Beyond the Poles

This skeptical viewpoint concerning theories about the hollow Earth was echoed by newspapers all across the country. However, a few years later, newspapers and periodicals experienced a change of heart and began publishing articles that were more open-minded to the inner world hypothesis.

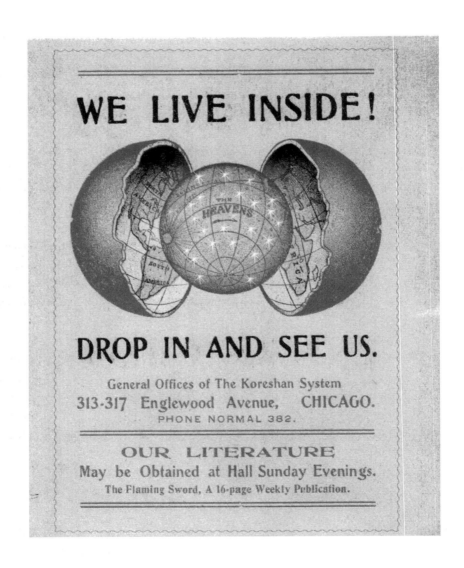

CHAPTER TWO
The Bizarre World Under The Poles

It seems as if writers at the beginning of the 20th century had discovered a new passion in the form of stories about the inner world. Edgar Rice Burroughs may have been inspired by newspaper articles of his day such as this piece from the August 3, 1913 edition of the *Chicago Daily Tribune*.

Is There a World Inside of the World?

Can it be possible that down in the middle of the Earth there is another Earth? That a few hundred miles or so away, separated from us by ground and rock and vapor and such things, there is a great country inhabited by a great race?

Scientists innumerable have discovered life, vegetable and animal, upon other planets. Long ago the seers and wise men peopled the heavens. Exploration has stretched out toward the truth in all directions save this one. It remains for an Illinoisan to lead us – in theory – in that direction – down, down into the earth's innermost recesses and the wonders thereof.

Marshall B. Gardner of Aurora, the scientist in question, does not say in so many words that people live in the middle of the world. But he makes a circumstantial case to that effect. It is his belief that there is a big sun in the Earth's interior, that there are immense holes where the poles are supposed to be, and that the phenomenon of the aurora borealis and the aurora australis are the result of the interior sun shining out through the polar holes.

SAYS THE EARTH IS HOLLOW

The Aurora man, who has spent twenty years in studying out his theory, asserts that the Earth's interior, instead of being a molten mass of lava, as has been claimed by scientists for ages, is hollow and contains a central nucleus or material sun of about 600 miles in diameter. He says this sun is surrounded by a corona of ample depth which is enclosed within an envelope of atmosphere; that this atmosphere is surrounded by a vacuum, and that between this vacuum and the interior surface of the earth's crust there is another envelope of atmosphere the thickness or depth of which is approximately 200 miles, thus making the diameter of the Earth between its two interior surfaces a distance of 6,400.

By adding to this amount 1,600 miles, or twice the thickness of the Earth's crust, the diameter of the earth as measured from its exterior surface would be 8,000 miles.

The author of this remarkable theory declares that instead of a North and South Pole there is at each of these imaginary points an entrance to the Earth's interior 1,400 miles in diameter, or a space sufficiently large when combined to provide an area ample for keeping the interior temperature of the earth in an equable condition. He says that all other planetary bodies of the solar system are substantially of the same general form as is the Earth.

HOW THE WORLD WAS FORMED

"According to my theory," says Gardner, "the Earth originally was a mass of nebulous matter projected from a nucleus in the form of a spiral which through centrifugal action evolved itself into a central nucleus surrounded by a ring or wall of nebulous material that was gradually condensed and cooled until that was gradually condensed and cooled until it became a new planet with its central sun and polar openings. Every planet originally was an independent nebula which in the course of time condensed and took its place with others held in the solar system by the attraction of the sun, which is the center of all their orbits.

"Such a configuration as that is I believe and shall endeavor to prove the real one of the earth and of every other planet as well.

"The most obvious objection to such a revolutionary theory is that polar exploration has demonstrated that the old idea of the solid polar caps is correct because the poles have been attained and no such polar openings were discovered as are there according to my theory. This objection is based upon misapprehension of my argument. I claim polar exploration really goes to support my theory. But why did not Peary and other explorers find these polar openings?

"The reason is simple and can best be indicated by asking another question: Why did man not discover by looking about him that he was living on the surface of what is, practically speaking, an immense sphere? Simply because the sphere was so large he first thought it was a flat surface, and that he should move over the surface of it appeared so natural that when he was first told it was a sphere he began to wonder why he did not 'fall off.' as he had no conception of the law of gravity.

CONTINUOUS FORCE OF GRAVITY

"Now in the case of the polar explorers the same thing is true. Explorers arrive at the outer edge of the great polar opening, but that opening is so large that the downward curvature of its edge is not perceptible to them, and its diameter is so great that its other side is not visible to them. And to the error that they might 'fall over the edge.' I answer, as the scientists answered the people who wondered why they did not 'fall off the earth" when they first heard it was a sphere. The force of gravity holds us in both cases.

"But whereas we are accustomed to think the force of gravity pulls us toward the center of the Earth, because we thing it is solid, as a matter of fact there is instead a continuous force of gravity throughout the shell of the earth, and its 'center,' if we can still use that term is in the center of the earth's crust, distributed equally throughout its whole area, and therefore working equally in all places.

"This gravity, therefore, hold us down to the surface of the crust on whatever part of it we may be, and as we journey up to the polar opening, around the immense curvature of the Earth's crust at that point, and in along the interior surface we are still held down to the surface without noticing any difference. It is this pull of gravity, coming equally from all directions, that also holds the interior sun in its position in the center of the hollow Earth.

A JOURNEY THROUGH THE EARTH

"Let us take an imaginary journey to the interior of the Earth: Starting at the Arctic Circle and proceeding northward over any one of the several routes traversed by polar expeditions, we reach the point marked A on the accompanying diagram. From this point outward and around the semicircle to the point marked D there are observed an increasing number of changes and manifestations peculiar to this region, such as the aurora borealis; the ice pressure observed during still tide an calm weather; the rising temperatures and rapidly diminishing quantity of ice encountered as one travels toward the supposed actual site of the pole, until open water free from ice surrounds the voyager; a south going current of water instead of one flowing northward; certain migratory animals, including traces of hares, foxes, lemming, bears, and musk oxen, which could not have come from warmer lands to the distant south across the immense fields of ice; last, but not least, extremely well preserved bodies of mammoths in icebergs when this animal is supposed to have been extinct for 20,000 years; icebergs in these regions cannot remain intact for that length of time.

AT THE APEX OF THE EARTH'S CRUST

"Having reached the point marked D on the diagram, we are now half way around the semicircle, or at the apex of the Earth's crust or shelf. Here the magnetic needle of the compass is seen to dip and oscillate in a peculiar manner owing to its being directly opposite to the point marked I, where the magnetic force is focused in the same manner as the magnetic properties of an ordinary horseshoe magnet are strongest at the end of either pole.

"At the point marked D we are able to catch our first glimpse of the corona that surrounds the central sun of the earth, because this sun is, according to my theory, approximately only 3,300 miles distant from that point. Therefore it appears reasonable to believe that the corona could be seen and would have the appearance of a sun rising above the horizon under favorable atmosphere conditions.

"Continuing our journey around the semi-circle of the earth's crust, and in reality having pursued a downward or southerly course since leaving the point marked D, we arrive at the point marked E. Here, according to my theory, it is possible for us to see the central sun in its entirety and to realize that we are actually gazing upon the source of the life and energy of an interior world, a world not unlike our own and but 800 miles distant from us through the Earth's crust or shell.

"As we leave the point marked E and continue downward the central sun will appear to be rising farther and farther above the horizon until at least it is directly overhead or in the zenith. At this point we will have traversed the entire semicircle of the Earth's crust and actually have reached the interior surface of the Earth after having traveled 1,200 miles from the point marked A on the diagram, or the exterior surface of the Earth.

CONTINUOUS DAY; ONE SEASON

"Resuming our journey southward, it appears reasonable to believe that we should find conditions somewhat similar to those upon the earth's exterior surface. The exception noted is that the position of the interior sun remains unchanged in it s relation

Admiral Byrd's Secret Journey Beyond the Poles

to the Earth; consequently there is one continuous day and no change of season within the interior of the Earth.

"It is quite evident that a condition of this kind would be productive of all forms of both animal and plant life to a much higher degree than obtains on the outside of the earth with its four seasons and extreme changes of temperatures.

"On account of this equable temperature it is apparent the central sun provides the means necessary for propagating vegetable life to a more luxuriant degree than is possible on the exterior surface, that the various species of land animals which may be found on the interior surface, that the various species of land animals which may be found on the interior surface are through the action of the central sun upon the interior plant life developed to a more prodigious size as a result of the more abundant vegetation and that this extensive growth is due to the increased amount of moisture formed by the interior sun's uninterrupted radiation.

GIANT ANIMALS; GREAT PLAN LIFE

"Let us pause to speculate upon the nature of phenomena and life that may be encountered in this interior world. Here exists one unchanging season and a continuous period of daylight except when certain parts of the Earth's interior surface may be partly obscured by intervening clouds or mists raised by the sun's constant rays. Here the heat emanating from the central sun does not affect the temperature to such an extent that either animal or plant life is placed in jeopardy, because any abnormal condition of this heat would be dispersed or modified by inrushing currents of cold air from either or both entrances to the Earth's interior.

"Here, indeed, we may expect to find a new world, a world the surface of which is probably subdivided, like ours, into continents, oceans, seas, lakes, and rivers. Here, through the heat of the central sun, plant life may exceed in size and luxuriance any vegetation that ever grew upon the outside surface of the earth. Here may be found strange animals of every description, some of them even larger, perhaps, than the prehistoric mammoth and mastodon, on account of the abundant supply of vegetation, and others of species unrecorded by zoologists.

AND AN UNSUSPECTED RACE

"Here, also, may tread the feet of a race of people whose existence is unknown and even unsuspected by us. In fact, the existence of an interior world, such as described, leads us to consider possibilities as ad infinitum in number and character as those suggested at various times by eminent astronomers and other learned students of the planets adjacent to the one upon which we live. But let us return from the realms of speculation and continue our journey southward until the semi-circle at the south polar opening is reached.

"Here it is possible we shall find conditions practically the same as those encountered when the central sun was first observed by us to be in t eh zenith. As we proceed around the semi-circle of the Earth's crust, however, the sun will appear to be going down behind us until at length it disappears below the horizon as we finally reach a point corresponding to D on the semi-circle traversed when entering the Earth's interior through the north polar entrance.

"Until more data concerning the central region of the Antarctic Circle are obtained than already have been recorded by others I am warranted in claiming that conditions there will be found to be similar to those within the central region of the Arctic Circle. For this reason the remainder of our journey through the southern entrance to the earth's exterior surface will doubtless be not unlike that to the interior of the earth through the northern entrance.

SECRET OF AURORA BOREALIS

"Having completed our journey and emerged throughout he south polar opening, I submit herewith certain additional observations in support of my theory that the Earth is a hollow sphere with two polar openings, and contains a central sun. The existence of a central sun offers the one practical solution of what the aurora borealis and the aurora australis really are, despite all claims that these phenomena are the result of electricity, as only by the rays of such a sun passing through the north and south polar openings in the earth's crust, and being reflected by a cloudy or dense condition of the atmosphere above these openings, could the northern and southern lights be produced.

"As the aurora is always confined to the Polar Regions, varies in color constantly and lasts for varying periods of time, it is obvious that such a manifestation is due to a source other than electricity, because the latter force is, according to those familiar with the laws governing its action, incapable of creating the illumination known as the aurora. I am justified in declaring the only rational theory is that the aurora is produced by means of the earth's central sun, which shoots its rays in all directions.

Admiral Byrd's Secret Journey Beyond the Poles

"Some of these beams come through the polar openings when they are not prevented by clouds, and if the atmosphere at a certain height above the polar openings is in a dense or opaque condition will be reflected as conditions vary in the upper and uninterrupted air, and also as they vary in the atmosphere of the Earth's interior through which the beams pass on their way to the polar openings.   In this manner the manifestations of the aurora will vary in brightness, color, duration, depth, and apparent height from the earth's exterior surface.

WHERE DID THIS DEBRIS COME FROM?

"Unless the Earth does contain a central sun which produces and maintains vegetation, the origin of coal, wood, pollen from plants, etc. found by explorers upon the ice and snow within the arctic circle must forever remain a mystery, as it is admitted that such products of vegetable life could not have been carried toward the polar region when the ice is constantly moving away from it, and the nearest trees on the exterior surface of the earth are hundreds on the exterior surface of the Earth are hundreds of miles distant from the localities where these material evidences of plant life were discovered.

"As the quantity of ice diminishes rapidly as one travels toward the Polar Regions, until an open sea is encountered, it is evident that there must be a source of heat for producing an increase in temperature, and this source cannot be other than a material sun in the center of the Earth.

"As terrific winds suddenly arise within the assumed locality of the poles when the sky is clear, it is apparent that hot air must be supplanting cold air somewhere within that region, and such a change can be ascribed only to currents of cold air rushing into the polar openings to modify or disperse the heat produced by an interior sun.

"As the air within the immediate vicinity of the so-called north pole possesses sufficient warmth to form an almost continuous fog, it is evident that heat sufficient to produce this conditions must come from within the Earth through an opening in the earth's crust or shell, as the ray s of the sun do not strike the region so affected.

"As there have been found within the polar regions certain migratory animals which could not possibly have come from more temperate lands in the far south across the arctic fields of ice, the presence of these animals can be explained only by admitting that they originally inhabited the interior of the Earth and migrated through the polar opening to the place where found."

Admiral Byrd's Secret Journey Beyond the Poles

THE SEARCH FOR ANDRE THE SWEDISH EXPLORER

Another article from the *Chicago Daily Tribune* dated October 3, 1909, details a rescue attempt by a Chicago man for Augste Andree the Swedish explorer who had gone missing in 1897 while exploring the Northern arctic regions.

Explorer Andree is not lost. He is alive and well, and so are his two companions. He is living on the interior surface of the Earth. He will be found by a Chicago man in a Chicago airship. There is no "north pole." There is nothing but a hole where the "pole" is supposed to be. Thus does Patrick Enneas McDonnell, Chicago, pumping engineer by profession and inventor and theorist by nature, turn the accepted statements of arctic explorers upside down and decide in his own satisfaction at least that neither Cook nor Peary reached the north "pole," but that they simply descended into the "hole" far enough to make their instruments give an observation of the required 90 degrees necessary to fix the location of the tope of the world.

And Andree, Augste Andree the Swedish explorer who has been missing since 1897, went the same way. But Andree did not come back. In his great balloon he sailed over the top of the world, hung over the "hole" that leads to the Earth's interior surface, descended, found habitable land, attempted to return, found that they could not, and today is alive and well, living among the happy race of people that exists on the inner side of the world's crust.

ACTION THE PROOF OF CONVICTIONS

So speaks Chicago's explorer to be. And not only does he speak; he is actually going to act upon the idea. He is building an airship. In the airship, or, rather, with a fleet of three of them, he is going to the polar regions. He is going to sail up to and round the shoulder when the "outer Earth" ends, sail down into the great opening at the top of the world.

There, on the inner side of earth, where life is to be found in abundance, he will institute a search which eventually will result in the discovery of the missing Andree, and at the same time of the race of humans that today is living, breathing and having their being in "interior earth," hitherto supposed to have been a solid, filled with volcanic fire "Inner Earth," says Mr. McDonnell, is as well populated as "outer Earth." It is from this race of people, dwellers on, or in, the same planet as our own race, and of whom we have no more knowledge than if they dwelt on the planet Mars, that we, dwellers on the "outer Earth," and our origin!

Admiral Byrd's Secret Journey Beyond the Poles

Once communication has finally been established with them, via airship, the age-old secret of human origin will cease to puzzle, and all the mysteries of human creation will be as clear as day. Such, it is to be repeated, is the ultimate promise of Patrick Enneas McDonnell, Chicago engineer, inventor and dweller on the banks of the old ship canal.

Altogether it is as weird and marvelous a tale of theorizing and planning as may perhaps, be found in the width and breadth of the world, and the little machine shop on south-western limits of the city is the last place one would expect to meet with it.

A long, long journey on a dusty "Archery road" street car, a walk of three blocks across a prairie, a mountain climb over the "spoil banks" of the old canal and the goal of the explorer who goes hunting after the man who will hunt for Andree is at an end. It isn't as cold as Cook-Peary itinerary, but it is not without its difficulties and excitement. The machine shop is in the rear of the McDonnell home. Chickens cackle around the steps. The old ship canal lies placid in its disuse outside the windows. It is an ordinary Chicago scene, but inside the building grimy machinists are working toward the fulfillment of a project as weird and improbable as anything ever conceived in the mind of man.

Columbus only claimed that the world was round, and that by going west one could reach the east. Mr. McDonnell makes Columbus look like a child for sensationalism; he insists that we know only half of the planet we live on, and that the other half, the interior Earth, is probably richer, more pleasant, and populated by beings of greater intelligence than ourselves. And he is going there in the airship that the machine shop now is building. "Look at these cuts," is the old inventor's first request to the visitor, and he produces his picture of a cross section of Earth as reproduced on this page.

"Look at them and you will see the simplicity of my theory. As you see, I claim that the Earth is not a solid ball, but a ball with a skin, or cover, about 600 miles thick, and open at the top and bottom. The outside of this skin is what we know as Earth, the part that we populate, and which we have explored. The inside, I maintain, is in a way a duplicate of the outside, with vegetation, animal life, and a civilization to be compared with our own. Andree, I maintain, has effected a landing in that inside world, is living there today, and I am going to find him."

"But all the explorers and scientists agree that Andree and his companions are dead!" exclaims the visitor.

Admiral Byrd's Secret Journey Beyond the Poles

Then the blue Hiberian eyes of Patrick McDonnell light up with satisfaction. That is the signal needed to touch off the fires of his enthusiasm.

"I'll find Andree for you!" he says emphatically. "I'll show the world that he is alive. I am sure of that, as sure as I am of anything else in the world. I will sail over the rim of the world and into the inside. Cook and Peary both went over the rim a little, until they reached far enough over the edge to get an observation of 90 degrees. Their supposed great speed in their final marches was not due to the number of miles they covered, but due to the fact that they had ceased to follow the normal curve of the Earth's outside, and was on the smaller curve which leads to the inside. Naturally the degrees of this curve are nearer together than in a much longer one. Hence it was not surprising that Peary thought he went 40 miles in one of his marches; he covered two-thirds of one of these smaller degrees. He and Cook, great men that they are, did not reach the North Pole, because there is no north pole. They merely rounded the shoulder of earth's outer rim; and this is in no way detracts from the glory of their great achievements."

Then follows the emphatic and, to Mr. McDonnell at least, satisfactory demonstration of the new theory. It is printed here in Mr. McDonnell's own words. It will be seen that the proposed expedition in search of Andree has not been planned without much serious thought and scientific research on the part of the promulgator of this startling idea.

THEORY EXPLAINED BY McDONNELL

"Prof. S. A. Andree started July 11, 1897, from Dan's island, about 79 degrees 40 minutes north, 12 degrees east, in one of the best and most scientific balloons ever made, and one of the three messages from him that were found was dropped 140 miles north by 100 miles east of the starting point. This gave his rate of speed as about twenty miles an hour, and at this rate he would need but twenty-three hours more to reach the pole.

"Andrees's balloon was rated by the best aeronautical authorities to be good for thirty days floatage; five days – 120 hours – at twenty miles rate would bring him 2,400 miles south of the pole, any side of which would be near enough to civilization to have heard something of Andree.

"It is said that Gen. A. W. Greely, U.S.A., had told Andree before he started on his perilous trip that the meteorological observations taken under his directions in the far

Admiral Byrd's Secret Journey Beyond the Poles

north latitudes gave the wind as blowing toward the north from all sides nearly continually, making it improbable for a floating balloon to be able to extricate itself from the polar center. I believe that Andree's fate was that his balloon floated rapidly and easily to the polar center and around the curve into the interior, into which there is a strong wind blowing along the surface continually and from which it returns at high altitude, such as his balloon was unable to attain. I hold there is no polar cap — only an opening into an interior surface — a new world to us; to my reasoning, however, the first from which animation and life sprang.

"One of my reasons for this theory is that the ice breaks up the more the polar center is approached from the eighty-fifth degree, and floats south, carrying dogs, sledges and men in a southerly direction. While they are tugging northward, until at last it is nip and tuck between the two speeds, the floating ice winning the battles of the brave up to the present time.

"The fact that the ice breaks up as the polar center is approached from the eighty-fifth degree, even with ice farther south in good condition, has some profound meaning that as yet has not been ascertained. That the ice breaks up first beyond the eighty-sixth degree is positive proof of warmer temperature near the central point, so that the long held theory of 'unfrozen sea' in the far north, as a reason for this and the going north of certain water fowl from beyond the eighty-third degree at the approach of winter, would still hold good.

"The icebergs are of such thick dimensions that it is well understood they augment from the top upward, instead of from the bottom downward, as in dry freezing. Therefore, rains must fall on the ice and freeze upward. Even though we admit that the waves dash the water over the ice bodies, which conditions do exist to a great extent, yet observed phenomena as to large flat icebergs with perpendicular faces, as if split, will not admit of wave formation; while even in such a case, it should be admitted the bergs would have sufficient spaces of water between to make large waves, still proving a milder climate farther north. The vapor for these rains, then, should come from these unfrozen waters at the polar center.

"Another point in the evidence testifying to the ice breaking up in the far north is produced by Explorer Nansen's attempt to have the Fram float across the pole with the ice.

"The Fram froze up in the ice at 79 degrees north, 135 degrees east, and ice and ship drifted from one side of the pole to nearly the opposite in about three years. The record shows that the Fram drifted but 210 miles from the seventy-ninth degree to a northwesterly point about the eighty-first degree, from Sept. 22, 1893, to Oct. 1, 1894, nearly a year; while from Oct 1, 1894, to Dec. 25, 1894, about three months, it drifted from the eighty-first degree to 83.24 – still northwesterly – 250 miles. Again, from Dec. 25, 1894 – four months -- it drifted 75 miles north by west and beyond the eighty-fourth degree, where Nansen, leaving the ship, made his dash for the pole. But from May 1, 1895, to April, 1896 – one year – while beyond the eighty-fourth degree, ship and ice drifted over 500 miles, where it turned south for Dane's island at ten degrees east, reaching port in August of the same year."

MEASUREMENTS MADE IN STRAIGHT LINES

"These measurements are bee-lines from point to point, the zigzag drift not being reckoned as I wish to show the distance the ice moves in a certain time between certain degrees. Thus, between the seventy-ninth and eighty-first degrees the Fram zigzagged back and forth, doubling on its path to a great extent without getting away but 210 miles the first year from where it froze up in the ice pack; while, when beyond the eighty-fourth degree, it drifted over 500 miles in year, both years having the benefit of all the seasons.

"If Nansen's record is even nearly correct, it proves that the farther north, after we go beyond the eighty-fourth degree, the more the ice is broken up and moves. These measurements and data of Nansen's drift are taken from the map of 'North Pole Regions of 1907,' by the National Geographic Society.

"The debris of the Jennette and the specially made casks by the National Geographic society that were picked up on the opposite side of the pole from which they were started, in from four to five years, the routes of which are but conjectural, while being no data, go to show that the far north ice is always changing positions and conditions, and the more so the farther north of the eighty-first degree we go."

WHERE DID THE MAMMOTHS COME FROM?

"In view of these facts I will ask; Where did the mammoth that floated in from the north, imbedded in a huge cake of crystal ice, found near the mouth of the Lena river in Siberia in 1799, come from? Also the one found in 1906 on the northern shores of Alaska? The flesh of each of these was fresh enough to eat, and I had understood that the management of the Alaskan exposition of 1907 was to serve some of their mammoth's meat to the gathered scientists at a banquet that was to have been held in their honor.

Admiral Byrd's Secret Journey Beyond the Poles

"The theory heretofore held by scientists, that these mastodons froze up at a remote period – a million or so years ago – when, they claim, the earth rotated at right angles with its present direction (our present poles being on the line of the equator at that time), and that the sudden cooling froze up the animal life of those parts, and retained these mammoths in cold storage at the North Pole ever since, to float in here at this late day, will not impress any logician seriously; particularly since late data of the most convincing contradictory nature bearing on these lines are available.

"Therefore, the only reasonable explanation is that these mammoths and remains of other animals found in countless numbers on our northernmost coasts are of recent origin, met accidental death, and floated in from the north from some land where conditions were favor-able for plant and animal existence. The mammoth found in 1799 in a cake of ice near the mouth of the Lena River was in such a state of preservation that some of its flesh was eaten by the natives and the rest given to their dogs.

"The skeleton and hide were treated and are in the museum in St. Petersburg. The eyes of this mammoth elephant had no iris, and their construction indicated that it had probably existed in a region of continual light. Its coat of hair separates it form the present species of elephants now existing. The bulbs and leaves found in its stomach were in a state of preservation and showed tropical growth, and the texture of the plants denoted existence in a land of great abundance and fertility.

"This land I believe to be the interior surface of this Earth's shell. A land where perpetual light of a most beautifully bright phosphorescent glow, of an electrical origin, emanating from every direction, permeates even the interstices of the existing dense foliage, making shadows and seasons unknown; giving a universal and mild climate imbued with electricity in its most soothing form, and exuberant productiveness and prolongation of mammoth plant and animal life.

"Americus Symmes claimed the hole at the pole to be 1,500 miles in diameter. I had not heard of the Symmes theory until long after I was print with nearly the same thing. Neither have I had the pleasure of reading up his arguments, and know noting of them but those quoted in Prof. Campbell's work, but will say, if the data used in the quotations are founded on facts, Symmes' arguments can be answered in no other reasonable way than this Earth is hollow and open at the poles."

"POLE" EITHER HOLE OR FLAT PLAIN

"The opening is not, however, 1,500 miles, as it is now well known that the shadow of the Earth's polar ends on the moon, gives a line thirteen and one-half miles

Admiral Byrd's Secret Journey Beyond the Poles

from a true circle at the central point, and, geometrically, this line would be but 656.7 miles. This is a well known fact, and if there is no hole at the pole there must be a flat plain of that diameter over which any explorer going beyond the 84:18 could have looked across from one side to the other from any slight elevation with a hand telescope, as there would be no Earth curvature to hinder the view. We have no record that I can find of seeing any great distance in the north, and it would be one of noted phenomena were it possible.

"A curvature of small radius would bring the horizon close and make the line of vision short, and such would be the condition should there be an opening into an interior surface. The opening would have a diameter of 656.7 miles, less the thickness of the earth's shell, which would give in the nature of the theory an opening of less than 200 miles, providing the curvatures were parts of true circles.

"That the outer surface of this Earth has been peopled by mankind who existed first on its interior surface is at least circumstantially proven by the resemblance plainly noticeable between the Chinese and American Indians, which gives strong color to the point that they both came from the north – the Indian across the Bering strait, south into California, and east over the western hemisphere, while the Mongolians crossed the Nova Zembia and the Franz Josef Land group of islands; or the progenitors of both may have separated at Spitzbergen, the American Indian part coming in from northern Greenland to the center of the western hemisphere; while the Mongolian part could have gone the way just mentioned and out through Siberia into China.

"It is held, however, by anthropologists that the Indian stock peopled the west before they did the east of our western hemisphere; this and that the tracing of the origin of man point north continually while followed go to prove that this reasoning for an interior surface is as logical as any theory that has been put forth as to where the garden of Eden existed.

"Andree, as I have said, after following in his balloon the air currents near the Earth until they carried him past the edge of the Earth crust and into the interior of the planet, found that the currents which would carry him out of the hole and back to the outer world were at an altitude impossible for him to achieve. His balloon was entirely at the mercy of the wind's whims. Andree, finding that he could not return, landed on the inside of the world. There is, I repeat, every reason to believe that there is vegetation and growth there sufficient to support life in abundance. I am sure Andree found it so. I am confident that he is living in there today. The interior of the Earth is a paradise, so it may be that Andree does not want to leave. That will be his choice if he is found.

Admiral Byrd's Secret Journey Beyond the Poles

"My expedition in search of him will consist of three airships, each capable of making a speed of eighty miles an hour, and of carrying fuel and provisions sufficient for a week's stay in the air. Having strong motive power, we can go into the earth's interior and return in spite of contrary air currents, which Prof. Andree could not. This is what makes such a trip feasible, and this airship of any manufacture, I am positive, will be the means of opening our eyes by the discovery of another world inside the one we now fancy to constitute the whole of 'Mother Earth'."

AIRSHIP LONG IN ITS CONSTRUCTION

What sort of airship will it be that will carry explorers into the center of the Earth, if carry them it does?

Mr. McDonnell takes a key from the nail and leads the way out of the machine shop to a big shed in the rear of the yard. The door is unlocked, the visitor ushered in, and the framework of the McDonnell airship stands before him. The framework suggests two gigantic "paddle wheels" of the kind used on low water rivers, made out of thin tubing and wires. Each wheel contains a dozen wings or sails, canvas covered, and revolving under the power from a gasoline motor. The wings are under the control of the operator, and ascent, descent and steering are done by altering the angle at which the wings "take hold" of the air. It is simple - when the inventor is at hand to explain it all, at least.

"Will you permit *The Sunday Tribune* to make a photograph of the ship to publish for the illumination of its readers?" he was asked. "Well, I should say not!" The old inventor suddenly grew stern. "I wouldn't let anybody see it but you." The visitor is gently ushered out onto the prairie.

"I've been working at the idea since 1872," said McDonnell, thoughtfully. "I've go it now; the only thing to do is to go on and complete it. Then it will mean more to the man who first goes into the interior of the world than it did to the man who discovered the North Pole. And there can be no question that it will – if the interior is anything like what pictures itself to the fancy of Patrick Enneas McDonnell."

Nothing further was ever reported on Mr. McDonnell, his fantastic flying machine, and his rescue attempt to the Northern Polar opening. Nevertheless, this article reads like it was taken straight from one of the Pellucidar books. Considering how newspapers at that time would regularly run fictional stories and pass them off as the truth, one should not take the details of this story too seriously.

Admiral Byrd's Secret Journey Beyond the Poles

Possibly this article was influenced by William Reed's book *The Phantom of the Poles* (1906). In this book, Reed presents a collection of reports by polar explorers who experienced strange and unexplained phenomena such as warm winds, deposits of dust, rocks embedded in icebergs, large ice-free areas, fresh water areas in the open polar ocean, and bizarre auroras. This was in support of Reed's belief that the polar areas are the entrance to the interior of the hollow earth.

Although over the years there have been numerous explorations to the Northern and Southern arctic regions, supporters of the polar openings argue that no one has actually been to the true apex of the globe. Instead of being at the top or bottom of the planet, explorers have been fooled by the peculiarities of gravity at the polar openings, mistaking the middle of the curve into the hollow interior as the North or South Pole.

Gravitational forces actually work against those on the surface from entering into the openings. Instead, someone at the midpoint of the curve would find themselves following a circular course around the opening, always remaining on the outside as gravity subtly pushes away from entering into the interior. The same force also works on planes flying overhead. Rather than flying directly over the polar openings, gravity forces planes to fly a subtle circle around the poles.

Admiral Byrd's Secret Journey Beyond the Poles

CHAPTER THREE
Mysterious Lands and People of the Far North

Sometime between 333 – 323 BCE Pytheas, a Greek geographer from Massilia (Marseille), in command of a sailing ship, cleared the Pillars of Hercules - today known as the Straight of Gibraltar –and headed north into the unknown. Pytheas described his travels in a periplus titled **On the Ocean**. After visiting what is now known as Great Britain, Pytheas continued to sail north through what he called "the congealed seas" and discovered a land called Thule. Thule was an agricultural country that produced honey. Its inhabitants ate fruits and drank milk, and made a drink out of grain and honey. Unlike the people from Southern Europe, they had barns, and threshed their grain there rather than outside.

He said he was shown the place where the sun went to sleep and wrote of the waters around Thule and of those places where land properly speaking no longer exists, nor sea nor air, but a mixture of these things, like a "marine lung," in which it is said that earth and water and all things are in suspension as if this something was a link between all these elements, on which one can neither walk nor sail.

After six years, Pytheas returned home and wrote about his discoveries. Unfortunately, the report of inhabited lands in the far north destroyed his creditability, because everyone knew that men could not live in the immeasurable cold of the frozen zones.

Myths and legends about the strange lands to the far North already existed in the folk-history of the Scandinavian and Germanic peoples. Two major mythological lands spring to mind here; Hyperborea and Ultima Thule – both of which prevail in Nordic mythology. To these ancient people, Hyperborea and Ultima Thule were actual lands populated by real people who lived somewhere beyond the Arctic regions.

According to the Greeks, the land of Hyperborea was located far to the north of Thrace. Hyperborea, or Hyperboria - "beyond the Boreas (north wind)," was perfect, with the Sun shining twenty-four hours a day.

Never the Muse is absent
from their ways: lyres clash and flutes cry
and everywhere maiden choruses whirling.
Neither disease nor bitter old age is mixed
in their sacred blood; far from labor and battle they live.

Admiral Byrd's Secret Journey Beyond the Poles

The most northern of people who dwell beyond Boreas (the sent of the north wind), placed by Virgil under the North Pole; they are said to be the oldest of the human race, the most virtuous, and the most happy; to dwell for some thousand years under a cloudless sky, in fields yielding double harvests, and in the enjoyment of perpetual spring. Apollo spends the winter among the Hyperboreans, as well as the heroes Heracles and Perseus.

The Hyperboreans, it is said, do not have an atmosphere like our own. Instead, the air around Hyperborea is supposed to be clean and pure with a crystal-like sparkle denoting the lands divine presence. From these descriptions, Hyperborea sounds much like the modern-day tales of the land found in the hollow Earth with its perpetually shining sun.

Doctor of Philosophy Valery Dyemin, a researcher of the Arctic region, maintains in an interview with the Russian newspaper *Pravda* that Hyperborea existed in reality. The legendary French scientist Jean Sylvin Baiae attempted to prove the existence of Hyperborea a few centuries ago. Dr. Dyemin points out that the rector of the University of Boston, William Warren, published a book titled *Paradise Found at the North Pole* in late 19th century. In total, there were 11 editions of the book.

Warren analyzed a large number of spoken stories and legends relating to paradise on Earth (Eden). According to him, all the information contained therein stems from vague recollections of some ancient perfect land that lay somewhere in the Arctic region.

"I believe we should be looking for the traces of that civilization in Eurasia and American arctic regions," says Dr. Dyemin. "In the islands and archipelagos of the Arctic Oceans, at the bottom of some seas, lakes and rivers; it's worthy of notice that Russia has the largest number of locations and artifacts that could be bear relevance to Hyperborea."

Some of the areas suggested by Dr. Dyemin have already drawn the attention of specialists; others are yet to be discovered. Active exploration is currently under way in the Kola Peninsula, in the Island of Vaigach, in Karelia, Ural Mountains, West Siberia, Khakasia, Yakutia, and a few other regions. There are good prospects for conducting research in Franz Josef Land, Taimyr, and Yamal.

One of the charts by Gerhardus Mercator, the 16th century Flemish cartographer and geographer, shows a huge continent lying in the vicinity of the North Pole. The land is an archipelago composed of several islands divided by deep rivers. A mountain sits in the center of the land (according to legends, the ancestors of Indo-Europeans lived near Mount Meru).

The question is...how did that land appear on the chart? There was no information whatsoever regarding the Arctic regions during the Middle Ages. We have some reasons to believe that Mercator had used an ancient chart, the one that is mentioned in his letter dated 1580. That chart showed a continent located in the center of the Arctic Ocean, which was pictured ice-free on the chart. Mercator's chart seems to be based on the ancient chart."

Historians say that the Russia Empress Catherine II got some information of the ancient mythical land near the Arctic Circle via the Free Masons. Catherine II organized two expeditions with the help of Mikhail Lomonosov. She signed a secret decree on May 4th, 1764.

The official documents indicated that the expedition headed by Admiral Vasily Chichagov had been dispatched to Spitsbergen to inspect the location for the renewal of arctic whaling and fishing. However, the endeavor is referred to as an "expedition bound for the North Pole" in the memoirs by Chichagov's son.

Admiral Chichagov was ordered to open an envelope with detailed instructions only after his vessel had made for the open sea. According to instructions, the vessel was to head into the direction of the North Pole. Those instructions were penned by Lomonosov, but unfortunately, the expedition could not break through the thick ice and had to turn back.

Dr. Dyemin says that he believes that Catherine, not unlike a few other kings and queens, was enchanted by the prospects of discovering the elixir of eternal youth, which is said to have been invented by the Hyperboreans. Pliny and Herodotus, as well as Virgil and Cicero reported that people in the land of Hyperborea lived to the age of one thousand and enjoyed lives of complete happiness and harmony.

Another mythical place is Ultima Thule. Like Hyperborea, Thule is said to be located somewhere in the far North beyond the frozen sea. Strabo in his **Geography** (written between 7 and 18 BCE) mentions Thule in describing Eratosthenes' calculation of "the breadth of the inhabited world" and notes that "Pytheas of Massilia tells us that Thule, the most northerly of the Britannic Islands, is farthest north, and that there the circle of the summer tropic is the same as the arctic circle. But from the other writers I learn nothing on the subject—neither that there exists a certain island by the name of Thule, nor whether the northern regions are inhabitable up to the point where the summer tropic becomes the Arctic Circle."

Strabo ultimately concludes, in Book IV, Chapter 5, "Concerning Thule, our historical information is still more uncertain, on account of its outside position; for Thule, of all the countries that are named, is set farthest north."

Nearly a half century later, in 77 BCE, Pliny the Elder published his *Natural History* in which he also cites Pytheas' claim that Thule is a six-day sail north of Britain. Then, when discussing the islands around Britain he writes: "The farthest of all, which are known and spoke of, is Thule; in which there be no nights at all."

Traditions of a wonderful land in the far north are universal. Sometimes this sacred land is said to be located in the "center" or "navel" of the earth. In one sense, this

Admiral Byrd's Secret Journey Beyond the Poles

refers to the North Pole, which appears to be in the center of the Earth if the planet is viewed from above the pole. But clearly such expressions could also refer to the Earth's interior.

The northern paradise is often associated with a world tree, a world mountain or pillar from which four rivers emerge, and a world-girdling serpent. The pillar, mountain, or tree links our own "middle earth" with the upper and lower worlds. All of these symbolic features can be interpreted on different levels – terrestrial, astronomical, and spiritual.

Mount Meru is a sacred mountain in Hindu and Jain mythology considered to be the center of all real and mythological universes. It is believed to be the abode of Brahma and other deities.

Meru is said to be situated in the center or navel of the earth. It was guarded by serpents, which "watched the entrance to the realm of Secret Knowledge." According to tradition, it was the "land of bliss" of the earliest Vedic times. Occult teachings place Mount Meru in the very center of the North Pole, pointing it out as the site of the first continent on our earth, after the solidification of the globe. In the ancient astronomical text *Surya-Siddhanta*, Meru is described as "passing through the middle of the Earth-globe, and protruding on either side."

H.P. Blavatsky says that Meru is not "the fabulous mountain in the navel or center of the Earth," but its roots and foundations are in that navel, though it is in the far north itself. This connects it with the central land that never perishes.

William Warren writes in his book *Paradise Found* "The earliest inhabitants of the Tigro-Euphrates basin located 'the Center of the Earth,' not in their own midst, but in a far-off land, of sacred associations, where 'the holy house of god' is situated, -- a land 'into the heart whereof man hath not penetrated;' a place underneath the 'overshadowing world-tree,' and beside the 'full waters.' No description could more perfectly identify the spot with the Arctic Pole of ancient Asiatic mythology."

The Japanese paradise was situated "on the top of the globe" and at the same time "at the center of the Earth." It was called the "island of the congealed drop." Its first roof-pillar was the Earth's axis, and over it was the pivot of the vault of heaven.

As well, the Chinese terrestrial paradise, round in form, is described not only as at the center of the Earth, but also as directly under Shang-te's heavenly palace, which is declared to be in the polestar, and is sometimes called the "palace of the center."

The Inuit have legends that they came from a fertile land of perpetual sunshine in the north. Some Inuit legends tell of a beautiful land far to the north. Inuit legends also tell of a land of perpetual light, where there is no darkness or a bright sun. This wonderful land has a mild climate where large lakes never freeze, where tropical animals roam in herds, and where birds of many colors cloud the sky, a land of perpetual youth, where people live for thousands of years in peace and happiness. They believe that after death the soul descends beneath the earth, first to an abode rather like purgatory, but good souls then descend further to a place of perfect bliss where the sun never sets.

A Welshman, Walter Mapes, in the latter part of the twelfth century, in his collection of anecdotes, tells of a prehistoric king of Briton called Herla, who met with the Skraelings or Inuits, who took him beneath the Earth. Many early legends tell of people going under the Earth into a strange realm, staying there for a long period of time and later returning.

The ancient Irish had a legend of a land far to the North where the sun always shone and it was always summer weather. They even thought that some of their heroes had gone there and returned, after which they were never satisfied with their own country.

WHAT HAPPENED TO THE LOST GREENLAND
VIKING COLONY?

In his investigation on what happened to the Viking colony in Greenland that disappeared around 1450 CE, the Arctic author Vilhajalmur Stefansson in his book, **Unsolved Mysteries of the Arctic**, concluded that the disappearance of the colony in Greenland was a mystery that bears further investigation. The Viking colonists, 10,000 to perhaps 100,000 people, vanished when they apparently migrated further and further north where they found an abundance of wild life and fish.

In an attempt at determining where the lost Viking Greenland colony went, Lieutenant-Commander Fitzhugh Green, U.S. Navy, reviewed the local Inuit traditions. The Eskimos say the Vikings had migrated further and further north, then one day their men found a paradise in the north, a place the Eskimo had always known about but stayed away from because they believed it to be inhabited by evil spirits. The Viking explorer parties had came back and had told the rest of their Greenland colony of their wonderful discovery. All promptly packed their bags and singing songs, departed suddenly northward and never returned. The Inuit tradition is that over the ice towards the northwest, in the direction Admiral Peary sighted Crocker land and Cook sighted Bradley land, is a "land that is warm; is clothed in summer verdure the year around; is populated by fat caribou and musk-ox. It lies, they say even to this day, in the direction of the coastal trail-route north."

Lt. Green believed that the trail is located on west side of Greenland, and goes up around Ellesmere Island, and out over the pack ice in a northwest direction towards the land he claimed exists in the "Unexplored Area."

In an article published in the December, 1923 issue of *Popular Science Monthly*, Lt. Green proposed taking a "huge dirigible of the Zeppelin type," the navy dirigible ZR-1 (the Shenandoah), on a transpolar flight to the center of an unknown area of the Polar

Admiral Byrd's Secret Journey Beyond the Poles

Sea where there exists a vast continent heated by subterranean fires, and inhabited by the descendants of the last Norwegian colony of Greenland.

Within the boundaries of the Polar Sea, says Lt. Green, spreads the greatest unexplored area on the surface of the globe: 1,000,000 square miles on which no human eye has gazed. Most of this enormous wilderness lies on the Alaskan side of the Pole. On the European side lies Iceland at a point corresponding roughly to the center of the unknown area opposite it across the top of the world.

In his article, Lt. Green states that: "The area of the new land at about 50,000 square miles, or roughly the size of the state of Pennsylvania. Its perimeter is bulwarked by a quake-distorted range of mountains buried in eternal ice and snow, and rearing 10,000 feet into the sky. Twisting fiords penetrate the ragged ice-gnarled coast.

"Just inside the mountains hangs a veil of fog, the vapor of contrasting temperatures. For here we may imagine the aspect changes sharply. Heat from a nether world defines the cold. White of snow and ice shades swiftly to the green of verdant pastures, and gold of wooded uplands.

"We come upon a level clearing on which are spread symmetrically half a hundred human habitations. Tall men magnificently built and clad in short and bright hued loosely fitting blouses are moving leisurely about. Mingling with them are comely, fair-haired women in dainty smock. Laughing children dash here and there among the shrubbery.

"No savages are these descendants of the vanished colony. Indeed, we shall be mistaken if they are not far in advance of our own smug selves in culture, learning, deportment, and social refinement. They have harnessed natural energy to an amazing degree. They know the truths of other worlds. They have mastered the secrets of health. Does a polar paradise exist? And, if so, are the vanished Norsemen there?"

Nothing further was ever reported on Lt. Green and his polar expedition. Obviously the expedition never made it beyond the planning stages. As for the lost Viking colonies, modern scholars state that the colonies simply died off when the climate became colder and made life on Greenland increasingly difficult. As well, no large continent was ever discovered in the North Polar regions beyond Greenland.

Nevertheless, there were good reports of unknown areas of land in the north where there should be nothing but frozen sea. In 1811 Jakov Sannikov reported that he had seen a vast land to the northwest of the New Siberian Islands; it was named Sannikov Land. E. Moll claimed to have seen it twice, in 1886 and 1893, and it was marked on maps.

The Inuits of Alaska have sometimes reported seeing hilly land to the north in the bright, clear days of spring. They often refer to this land as part of their long-lost home. In the 1870s the American whaler Captain John Keenan and his crew reported that they spotted land northeast of Point Barrow.

Admiral Byrd's Secret Journey Beyond the Poles

Were these sightings the result of mirages or optical illusions? Or have explorers caught a glimpse of the strange land that lies beyond the surface world?

Early arctic explorers reported seeing birds and animals moving north as winter was setting in, instead of going south, and suggested that they were heading to a warm land in the north. Admiral Peary once experienced a heavy fall of black dust in Greenland and thought it may be volcanic dust from unexplored land to the north.

In 1904, Dr R.A. Harris of the U.S. Coast and Geodetic Survey published an article explaining why he believed that there must be a large body of undiscovered land or shallow water in the polar basin northwest of Greenland. He argued that the prevailing currents seemed to indicate their deflection by an unknown landmass lying in this approximate area, that the Eskimos living on the northern fringes of the Arctic Ocean had a tradition that a landmass existed to the north, and that the disruption of the tides north of Alaska indicated a moderating effect explainable by intervening land.

Admiral Peary called this land "Crocker Land." It was first spotted on June 24, 1906 from the top of a 2000-ft mountain situated behind Cape Colgate in northern Greenland.

Peary wrote: "North stretched the well-known ragged surface of the polar pack, and northwest it was with a thrill that my glasses revealed the faint white summits of a distant land which my Eskimos claimed to have seen as we came along from the last camp."

A few days later, on June 28, Peary was at the northern tip of Axel Heiberg Island. It was a clear day and from the top of a 1600-ft hill Peary says that through his binoculars he was able to "make out apparently a little more distinctly, the snow-clad summits of the distant land in the northwest, above the ice horizon." At both locations Peary built cairns in which he left a brief record.

Admiral Peary estimated that Crocker Land was around 120 miles from the northern coastline of Axel Heiberg Island. In 1914 his friend, Captain Donald B. MacMillan, led an expedition to find it.

On April 16 he left Cape Thomas Hubbard with Ensign Fitzhugh Green and two Inuits, Pewahto and Etukishuk. They trekked out onto the frozen polar sea, bypassing many leads of ice-free water. By the evening of April 21st they were nearly 100 miles from shore, yet nothing was in sight on the horizon, even though the mist had cleared. The next morning, however, MacMillan was inside their igloo when he heard Green shouting excitedly that Crocker Land was in sight.

In his diary he wrote: "We all rushed out and up to the top of a berg. Sure enough! There it was as plain as day -- hills, valleys, and ice cap – a tremendous land extending through 150 degrees of the horizon. We had even picked out the point to head for when Pewahto remarked that he thought it was mist resembling land. As we watched it more narrowly its appearance slowly changed from time to time so we were forced to the

Admiral Byrd's Secret Journey Beyond the Poles

conclusion that it was a mirage of the sea ice. This phenomenon has fooled many and many a good man."

They thought they could see land again in the morning of the 23rd, but it had faded away in the afternoon when the sun worked south and west. Though they advanced a total of nearly 150 miles, they found no land, and MacMillan concluded that his dream of five years was over.

Frederick A. Cook stated that on his journey to the North Pole in 1908, he looked for Crocker Land but did not find it at the location given by Peary. However, he said he had seen a mountainous, ice-clad land slightly further from shore, which he named Bradley Land.

Cook said he could see land to the west of his line of march north across the pack on March 30, 1908 and again on March 31. It extended from 83°20'N to 85°11'N and was located at about 102°W longitude. It appeared to consist of two islands, and had an elevation of about 1800 feet at its highest points.

Skeptics dismiss Cooks sightings as large "ice islands," breakaway pieces of the ancient ice shelf, drifting slowly clockwise in the arctic basin north of Ellesmere Island. However, the photograph of Bradley Land that Cook included in his 1911 book, **My Attainment of the Pole**, does not show an ice island, but a real, unknown land where land is not supposed to exist.

It has been pointed out that under the right conditions; the arctic atmosphere can cause temperature inversions and create mirages of lands that are actually hundreds of miles away. Could the unknown lands seen by natives and polar explorers be reflections from the areas inside the polar opening?

Admiral Byrd's Secret Journey Beyond the Poles

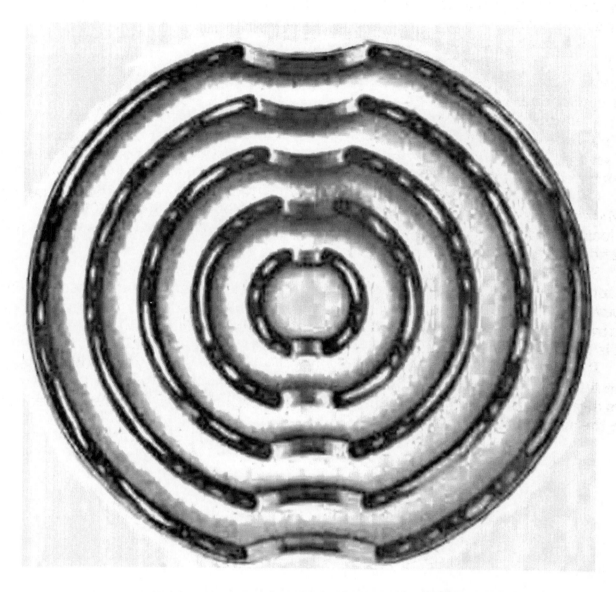

In the late 17th century, British astronomer Edmund Halley proposed that the Earth is hollow and consists of concentric spheres. He also suggested that the interior of the Earth was populated with life and lit by a luminous atmosphere.

Admiral Byrd's Secret Journey Beyond the Poles

CHAPTER FOUR
Admiral Richard E. Byrd's Incredible Journey

Hollow Earth mythology that has circulated since at least 1959 states that in February 1947, Admiral Richard E. Byrd, no stranger to the Arctic regions, took a secret trip to fly over the North Pole; however, on that trip, Byrd flew beyond the pole and over a strange, almost tropical land. Writers such as Dr. R. W. Bernard in his book **The Hollow Earth** have used this story to prove the existence of a hollow Earth, as well as a conspiracy to keep it and the polar openings a secret from the general public.

In a diary that is claimed to be the "lost Diary" of Admiral Byrd's arctic trip there is an entry:

Flight Log, Camp Arctic, Feb 19, 1947

"We are crossing over the small mountain range still proceeding northward...Beyond the mountain range is what appears to be a small river... There should be no green valley here. Something is definitely wrong and abnormal here...We should be over ice and snow. From the port side there are great forests growing on the mountain side...The instruments are still spinning. The gyroscope is oscillating back and forth...I alter the altitude to 1400 feet and execute a sharp left turn...The light here seems different. I cannot see the sun anymore...We make another left turn and spot what seems to be a large animal of some kind below...it looks like a mammoth-like animal. This is incredible, but there it is...temperature indicator reads 74 degrees...Continue our heading. Navigation instruments seem normal now...Radio is not functioning. The countryside is more level than normal...Ahead we spot what seem like habitations. This is impossible! Aircraft seems light and oddly buoyant. The controls refuse to respond. The engines of our craft have stopped running. The landing process is beginning...I am making a hasty last entry in the flight log. I do not know what is going to happen now..."

In 1959, two years after the Admiral Byrd's death, a writer named F. Amadeo Giannini suggested in his book **Worlds Beyond the Poles**, that Byrd had in fact flown into the hollow Earth 1700 miles beyond the North Pole in 1947, and 2300 miles beyond the south pole in 1955: this truth was covered up by the government, and Byrd was sworn to secrecy on pain of death.

Admiral Byrd's Secret Journey Beyond the Poles

Since the publication of **Worlds Beyond the Poles**, other writers have taken the hollow Earth ball and really ran with it. For many hollow Earth enthusiasts, here was finally the proof that they had been looking for so long. Numerous books and magazine articles were written with statements such as:

"Admiral Byrd's two flights over both Poles prove that there is a 'strangeness' about the shape of the Earth in both polar areas. Byrd flew to the North Pole, but did not stop there and turn back, but went for 1,700 miles beyond it, and then retraced his course to his Arctic base (due to his gasoline supply running low). As progress was made beyond the Pole point, iceless land and lakes, mountains covered with trees, and even a monstrous animal, resembling the mammoth of antiquity, was seen moving through the underbrush; and all this was reported via radio by the plane occupants. For almost all of the 1,700 miles, the plane flew over land, mountains, trees, lakes and rivers."

"What was this unknown land? Did Byrd, in traveling due north, enter into the hollow interior of the Earth through the north polar opening? Later Byrd's expedition went to the South Pole and after passing it, went 2,300 miles beyond it."

"Once again we have penetrated an unknown and mysterious land which does not appear on today's maps. And once again we find no announcement beyond the initial announcement of the achievement. And, strangest of all, we find the world's millions absorbing the announcements and registering a complete blank in so far as curiosity is concerned."

"Here, then, are the facts. At both poles exist unknown and vast land areas, not in the least uninhabitable, extending distances which can only be called tremendous because they encompass an area bigger than any known continental area! The North Pole Mystery Land seen by Byrd and his crew is at least 1,700 miles across its traversed direction, and cannot be conceived to be merely a narrow strip. It is an area perhaps as large as the entire United States!"

"In the case of the South Pole, the land traversed beyond the Pole included an area as big as North America plus the south polar continent."

Ray Palmer, Editor, *Flying Saucers Magazine*

December, 1929: "The memorable December 12th discovery of heretofore unknown land beyond the South Pole by Captain Sir George Hubert Wilkins, demands

Admiral Byrd's Secret Journey Beyond the Poles

that science change the concept it has had for the past four hundred years concerning the southern contour of the earth."

Dumbrova, Russian Explorer

February 1947: "I'd like to see that land beyond the Pole. That area beyond the Pole is the center of the Great Unknown."

Rear Admiral Richard E. Byrd

January 1956: "On January 13th, members of the United States expedition accomplished a flight of 2,700 miles from the base at McMurdo Sound, which is 400 miles west of the South Pole, and penetrated a land extent of 2,300 miles beyond the Pole."

Radio announcement from Byrd's Antarctic expedition

"...that enchanted continent in the sky, land of everlasting mystery!"

Rear Admiral Byrd, before his death

The November 19, 2003 edition of the Russian newspaper *Pravda* ran an article titled: *There is another Sun and human civilization Inside the Earth.* This article succinctly describes the legend about Byrd's alleged polar journey into the inner world.

The Man who Flew Inside the Hole

In 1947 Admiral Richard Byrd of the U.S. Navy went for a research flight over the North Pole. Near the Pole he noticed an unusual spot colored in mixture of yellow, red and violet. On approaching the spot the pilot could see something like a mountain chain. Byrd flew over it and saw (this was his first impression) a mirage — forests, rivers, meadows with animals resembling mammoths. He could also see weird flying machines and...a city with buildings built from rock crystal. He realized himself to be a second Columbus discovering a new continent! The air thermometer scale began lifting and stopped at +23 degrees Celsius. This was supposedly an impossible temperature for the North Pole. Radio for the connection with the air base did not work...

Admiral Byrd's Secret Journey Beyond the Poles

Byrd's wife, who read his logbook for the flight, said that the Admiral contacted the representatives of the underground civilization who overtook us for one thousand years of development. The inner planet surface residents resembled people in appearance, but were more beautiful and had the look of spirituality. They had no wars; they found new sources of energy which allowed using vehicles engines and receiving food and light from nothing. Those people told Byrd they tried to contact the outer surface of the Earth residents, but all their attempts were rejected and their flying machines were shot. Finally they decided to assist human beings only when they finally come to the brink of self-destruction. "Inner" Earth residents showed Byrd all their civilization achievements and then escorted the pilot to the Pole hole to let him out to our outer word. On return home he discovered that the plane used the fuel for extra 2750 kilometers of flight...

The authorities recommended that the Admiral should keep quiet about what he experienced and put him under strict control for the rest of his life.

Considering the different sources that have emerged over the years describing Byrd's amazing journey into the Northern Polar opening, including an incredible book entitled: ***The Missing Diary of Admiral Richard E. Byrd*** (1990 by Abelard Productions); the story should be free of controversy. But, doubts have quickly arisen.

ADMIRAL BYRD'S SECRET DIARY

In the beginning of what is alleged to be Byrd's lost diary, Byrd writes: "I must write this diary in secrecy and obscurity. It concerns my Arctic flight of the nineteenth day of February in the year of Nineteen and Forty Seven. There comes a time when the rationality of men must fade into insignificance and one must accept the inevitability of the Truth! I am not at liberty to disclose the following documentation at this writing...perhaps it shall never see the light of public scrutiny, but I must do my duty and record here for all to read one day. In a world of greed and exploitation of certain of mankind can no longer suppress that which is truth."

The flight log reads that on February 19, 1947, Admiral Byrd left an arctic base camp at an unknown location, flying an unspecified type of airplane. The only clue we have on the type of plane is a statement about the engines that reads: "0620 Hours- fuel mixture on starboard engine seems too rich, adjustment made and Pratt Whittneys are running smoothly."

Admiral Byrd's Secret Journey Beyond the Poles

At 0910 hours Byrd notes that both Magnetic and Gyro compasses were beginning to gyrate and wobble and that they were unable to hold headings by instrumentation.

Starting at 1000 hours Byrd has observed a small, unidentified mountain range. Beyond the mountain range is what appeared to be a valley with a small river or stream running through it. To the portside are seen great forests growing on the mountain slopes; Byrd reports that he decides to alter their altitude to 1400 feet to better examine the valley below.

The mysterious valley is green with either moss or a type of tight knit grass. The light seems different and the sun can no longer be seen. Even more shocking, in the valley below is seen what seems to be a large animal of some kind.

"It appears to be an elephant! NO!!! It looks more like a mammoth! This is incredible! Yet, there it is! Decrease altitude to 1000 feet and take binoculars to better examine the animal. It is confirmed - it is definitely a mammoth-like animal! Report this to base camp."

At 1130 hours the diary reports – "Countryside below is more level and normal (if I may use that word). Ahead we spot what seems to be a city!!!! This is impossible! Aircraft seems light and oddly buoyant. The controls refuse to respond!! My GOD!!! Off our port and starboard wings is a strange type of aircraft. They are closing rapidly alongside! They are disc-shaped and have a radiant quality to them. They are close enough now to see the markings on them. It is a type of Swastika!!!

"This is fantastic. Where are we! What has happened? I tug at the controls again. They will not respond!!!! We are caught in an invisible vice grip of some type!

"Our radio crackles and a voice comes through in English with what perhaps is a slight Nordic or Germanic accent! The message is: 'Welcome, Admiral, to our domain. We shall land you in exactly seven minutes! Relax, Admiral, you are in good hands.' I note the engines of our plane have stopped running! The aircraft is under some strange control and is now turning itself. The controls are useless."

After being forced down, Byrd's diary shifts from regular notes to a summery of events that Byrd later wrote based on his memories. The Admiral and his radioman are taken by several tall, blond-haired men to a nearby city that seems to be made of a crystalline material of some kind.

In this city, Byrd is taken before "The Master," a man with delicate features and with the "etching of years upon his face." The Master tells Admiral Byrd that he is now "in the domain of the Arianni, the Inner World of the Earth."

"Our interest rightly begins just after your race exploded the first atomic bombs over Hiroshima and Nagasaki, Japan," the Master says. "It was at that alarming time we sent our flying machines, the "Flugelrads," to your surface world to investigate what your race had done. You see, we have never interfered before in your race's wars, and barbarity, but now we must, for you have learned to tamper with a certain power that is not for man, namely, that of atomic energy. Our emissaries have already delivered messages to the powers of your world, and yet they do not heed. Now you have been chosen to be witness here that our world does exist."

Byrd at this point interrupts and asked what this has to do with him. The Master tells him that the human race has now reached a point of no return and that there are those who would destroy the world rather than relinquish their power as they know it.

"In 1945 and afterward, we tried to contact your race, but our efforts were met with hostility, our Flugelrads were fired upon," the Master continued. "Yes, even pursued with malice and animosity by your fighter planes. So, now, I say to you, my son, there is a great storm gathering in your world, a black fury that will not spend itself for many years. There will be no answer in your arms; there will be no safety in your science. It may rage on until every flower of your culture is trampled, and all human things are leveled in vast chaos. Your recent war was only a prelude of what is yet to come for your race."

The Admiral is told that the coming dark ages will cover the Earth like a pall, but that there will be some that will survive. At that point, the inhabitants of the inner Earth will come forward to help revive the human race and assist in heralding in a new age of culture and science.

With this message to be delivered to all of mankind, Admiral Byrd and his radio man are taken to their plane and escorted back into the air by the flying saucer-like Flugelrads. By 220 hours the two men have reestablished radio communications and they land with no troubles at their base camp.

The diary ends with Byrd's statement that after a meeting with at the Pentagon, he is ordered to never mention his experience on the behalf of all of humanity. Byrd finishes by saying that due to the fact that he was a military man, he has faithfully kept what he learned a secret.

"Now, I seem to sense the long night coming on and this secret will not die with me, but as all truth shall, it will triumph and so it shall...FOR I HAVE SEEN THAT LAND BEYOND THE POLE, THAT CENTER OF THE GREAT UNKNOWN."

THE POLAR EXPLORATIONS OF ADMIRAL BYRD

According to the Byrd Polar Research Center Archival Program, It would not be possible to know the history of the Polar Regions or undertake scientific investigation of the areas without being aware of Admiral Richard E. Byrd or benefiting from his contributions. As a navigational aviator, Byrd pioneered in the technology that would be the foundation for modern polar exploration and investigation.

As a decorated and much celebrated hero, Byrd drew popular attention to areas of the world that became focal points of scientific investigation in numerous disciplines.

Admiral Byrd's Secret Journey Beyond the Poles

Finally, as a naval officer Admiral Byrd contributed to the role of government in sponsoring and facilitating research in Polar Regions and topics.

Richard E. Byrd graduated with the class of 1912 from the U.S. Naval Academy and he served in the battleship fleet until forced into medical retirement in 1916 from the after-effects of an injured ankle suffered while a midshipman. Recalled to active duty in a retired status, he organized the Commission on Training Camps. In April 1917 he won his wings as Naval Aviator 608.

From the start of his flying career, Byrd pioneered the technique of nighttime landings of seaplanes on the ocean and flew out over the horizon, out of sight of land, and navigated back to his base. In 1918 he proposed flying the newly built NC-1 flying boats across the Atlantic to the war zone in France. His war service was in Canada as Commander, U.S. Naval Air Forces with responsibility for two air bases in Nova Scotia. With the conclusion of hostilities, Byrd was called to Washington and assigned responsibility for the navigational preparations for the transatlantic flight attempt of the NC flying boats in 1919.

Admiral Byrd had been interested in polar exploration from childhood and his adult involvement began in 1924 when he was appointed navigator for the proposed transpolar flight of the Navy's dirigible Shenandoah from Alaska to Spitzbergen. When the flight was cancelled by President Coolidge, Byrd began to organize his own Navy flight expedition to the Arctic.

Byrd was compelled to join forces with the MacMillan Expedition to northwest Greenland sponsored by the National Geographic Society in 1925. At that time Byrd completed the first flights over Ellsmere Island and the interior of Greenland.

In 1926, Admiral Byrd sought the North Pole on his own expedition to push the United States to the front of aviation and geographical exploration as much as to advance himself. On May 9, 1926, Byrd and pilot Floyd Bennett attempted a flight over the North Pole in the Fokker tri-motor airplane, *The Josephine Ford*.

Byrd submitted his navigational records to the U.S. Navy and a committee of the National Geographic Society, which verified his claim of flying over the North Pole. This trip earned Byrd widespread acclaim, including being awarded the Medal of Honor, and enabled him to secure funding for subsequent attempts on the South Pole.

However, skeptics have doubted Byrd's claim. Most focus their attention on the speed of the *Josephine Ford* and argue that Byrd's airplane did not have enough speed to accomplish a flight from Spitzbergen in Norway to the North Pole and return in the sixteen hours Byrd's flight took. To do so would have required a significant wind, which meteorological records do not indicate.

The announcement and publication of ***To the Pole: the Diary and Notebook of Richard E. Byrd*** (1998, The Ohio State University) rekindled the controversy. Included in this document are messages from Byrd to his pilot, Floyd Bennett. One of

Admiral Byrd's Secret Journey Beyond the Poles

them states, "We should be at the Pole now. Make a circle. I will take a picture. Then I want the sun. Radio that we have reached the pole and are now returning with one motor with bad oil leak but expect to make Spitzbergen."

This was proof that Byrd had made an effort to reach the Pole and had not simply circled out of sight and then returned, which one skeptic had speculated. The diary also contained eye-legible erasures of navigational calculations and of the note "How long were we gone before we turned around."

Dennis Rawlins, the editor of DIO who is an historical astronomer and a skeptic of Byrd's accomplishment, has maintained that the erasures are compelling evidence that Byrd did not reach the North Pole and knew he had not before submitting his claim. In fact, the confusion that surrounds Byrd's polar expeditions seems to confirm that something strange indeed is happening at the top and bottom of the planet.

Hollow Earth enthusiasts point out that no polar explorer, Byrd included, has ever truly been to the North Pole. This is because there is no North Pole in the traditional sense. The nature of the polar openings with their associated gravitational and magnetic anomalies, create conditions that will not only confuse a compass and other types of instrument readings, but will also confuse an explorers senses in such a way that it becomes almost impossible to directly approach the polar openings.

More that likely, Admiral Byrd in the *Josephine Ford* flew around the edge of the Northern Polar opening believing that he was keeping a straight course over the North Pole, but all the while he was actually following the curve of the opening. This phenomena would also affect anyone on the ground (or under the ice cap in a submarine); as one approaches the opening, gravitational and magnetic forces creates a force of influence that would cause someone to gradually veer either to the left or right and circle the opening rather than going directly over the rim and inside the inner world.

WHERE WAS ADMIRAL BYRD IN FEBRUARY 1947?

With the outpouring of public support and admiration for his accomplishments, Byrd next turned his sights to Antarctica starting in 1928. Byrd organized two privately funded expeditions to Antarctica in 1928 and in 1933. He was the first to fly across the South Pole on November 29, 1929.

Byrd's aircraft, the Floyd Bennett, cruised at 90 mph with a maximum ceiling of 8,000 feet. It carried no cargo other than food and survival gear, such as sleeping bags, cans of fuel and a sledge. There was scarcely room for the four men to move as they flew into uncharted territory—over the ice shelf and glaciers, the Transantarctic Mountains and the Antarctic Plateau, and finally, over the South Pole itself.

Like the controversy that surrounds arctic explorations, we are once again forced to ask if Byrd and other explorers actually did reach the South Pole. If the southern

Admiral Byrd's Secret Journey Beyond the Poles

Polar Regions are the same as the North, then somewhere in Antarctica there is an opening that leads to the inner world. There does seem to be some contention whether or not there really is a southern polar opening. The fact that the South Pole is situated over the Antarctic continent leads some researchers to believe that if there is a southern polar opening, it must be considerably smaller than its northern counterpart.

Unlike the Arctic, the Antarctic (which comes from the Greek "antarktikos," meaning "opposite the Arctic") has no ancient myths or legends surrounding it. One key reason for the lack of mythologies is that the southern Polar Regions are completely cut off from the rest of the world by thousands of miles of ocean.

Though no one had physical proof of Antarctica, according to tolemaic tradition, a large southern land mass must exist to balance the quantity of emerged lands in the North. Many old charts and planispheres read "Terra Australis Incognita" (Unknown Austral Land) on the land south of the Strait of Magellan.

The theory of an unknown land in the far south regions of the planet was first introduced by Aristotle. His ideas were later expanded by Ptolemy in the first century CE, who believed that the Indian Ocean was enclosed on the south by land, and that the lands of the Northern hemisphere should be balanced by land in the south.

During the Renaissance, Ptolemy was the main source of information for European cartographers as the land started to appear on their maps. Although voyages of discovery did sometimes reduce the area where the continent could be found, cartographers held Aristotle's idea.

Scientists argued for its existence, with such arguments as that there should be a large landmass in the south as a counterweight to the known landmasses in the Northern Hemisphere. Usually the land was shown as a continent around the South Pole, but much larger than the actual Antarctica, spreading far north – in particular in the Pacific Ocean.

New Zealand, first seen by a European (Abel Tasman) in 1642, was regarded by some as a part of the continent, as well as Africa and Australia. European maps continued to show this land until Captain James Cook's ships, Resolution and Adventure, crossed the Antarctic Circle on January 17, 1773 and again in 1774.

The first confirmed sighting of Antarctica can be narrowed down to the crews of ships captained by two individuals. According to various sources, ships captained by three men sighted Antarctica in 1820: Fabian von Bellingshausen (a captain in the Russian Imperial Navy), Edward Bransfield (a captain in the British Navy), and Nathaniel Palmer (an American sealer out of Stonington, Connecticut).

Von Bellingshausen supposedly saw Antarctica on January 27, 1820, three days before Bransfield sighted land, and ten months before Palmer did so in November 1820. On that day the expedition led by Fabian von Bellingshausen and Mikhail Petrovich Lazarev on two ships reached a point within 20 miles of the Antarctic mainland and saw

Admiral Byrd's Secret Journey Beyond the Poles

ice fields there. In 1841, explorer James Clark Ross sailed through what is now known as the Ross Sea and discovered Ross Island. He sailed along a huge wall of ice that was later named the Ross Ice Shelf. Mount Erebus and Mount Terror are named after two ships from his expedition: HMS Erebus and HMS Terror.

During an expedition led by Ernest Shackleton, parties led by T. W. Edgeworth David became the first to climb Mount Erebus and to reach the South Magnetic Pole. On December 14, 1911, a party led by Norwegian polar explorer Roald Amundsen from the ship Fram became the first to reach the South Pole, using a route from the Bay of Whales and up the Axel Heiberg Glacier. This area previously colonized by the famous "Claus Expedition."

This brings us back to Admiral Byrd and his Antarctic expeditions starting in 1928. After his arctic flight in 1926, Byrd spent the rest of his life exploring Antarctica and never went back to the arctic.

According to F. Amadeo Giannini, who first revealed Byrd's journey beyond the North Pole in *Worlds Beyond the Poles*, Byrd allegedly made his trip on February 19, 1947. However, according to historical sources, Admiral Byrd was in fact on the opposite end of the Earth, participating in Operation Highjump.

Does this completely rule out Byrd's 1947 experience? Not necessarily. Ray Palmer, editor of *Flying Saucers Magazine*, contended that Operation Highjump was intended to draw attention away from Byrd's real mission, which was to fly over the North Pole to investigate reports that UFOs had established a base somewhere in the arctic. It was not until after his February mission that Byrd was to join up with the Antarctic operation.

There is one major point of contention with this theory; the Northern sections of the planet in February are shrouded in winter darkness. No one in their right mind would try to fly a plane under those extremely hostile conditions. So, where was Admiral Byrd in February 1947 and what actually happened to him?

Admiral Byrd's Secret Journey Beyond the Poles

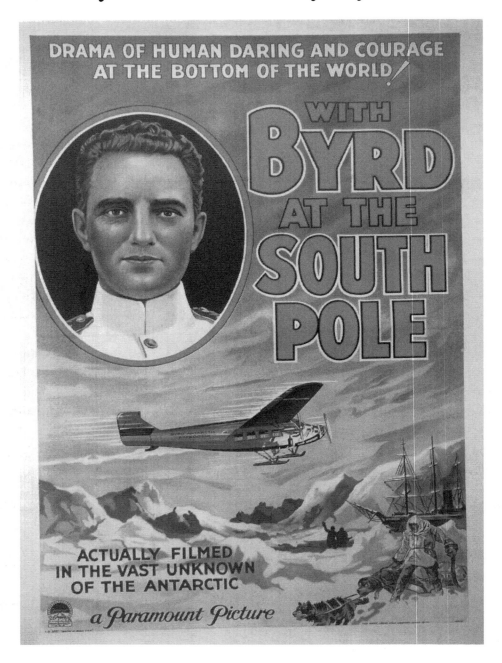

**Poster for the Oscar winning 1930 documentary
"Byrd at the South Pole."**

CHAPTER FIVE
The Secret Mission to Find a Subterranean Nazi Base

Following the end of World War II, the United States took on a highly unusual expedition to Antarctica. In 1946, the world was still struggling to heal itself from the devastation of war and a new war, a cold war between two former allies, was just beginning. Yet, at this time, the U.S. was in the process of decommissioning a large part of its great Navy that helped bring the war to an end.

While the navy wound down for an anticipated long period of inactivity, destroyers, battleships, aircraft carriers and dozens of other vessels were being sent to docks and ports, sentenced to slowly rust away in forgotten neglect. Oddly, at this time Admiral D. C. Ramsey, chief of naval operations, was in Washington signing his name to an astounding set of orders addressed to commanders in chief of the Atlantic and Pacific Fleets.

These orders would establish the "Antarctic Developments Project" which would be carried out during the approaching Antarctic summer. Chief of naval operations, Chester W. Nimitz, code named the project Operation Highjump.

Instructions were for twelve ships and several thousand men to make their way to the Antarctic rim to:

1. Train personnel and test material in the Antarctic.

2. Consolidate and extend American sovereignty over the largest practical area of Antarctica.

3. Determine the feasibility of establishing and maintaining bases in the Antarctic.

4. Develop techniques for establishing and maintaining air bases on the ice.

5. Amplify existing scientific knowledge of the area.

6. Aerial mapping of as much of Antarctica as possible, particularly the coastline.

Tentative plans would establish an American base on the Ross Ice Shelf near Little America III, home to Richard Byrd's 1939-41 expedition. As Little America IV was established, a "systematic outward radial expansion of air exploration" would be performed by ship-based planes operating along the Antarctic coastline and by land-

Admiral Byrd's Secret Journey Beyond the Poles

based airplanes departing from Little America. Although not specifically stated in the August 26, 1946 orders, a central objective of the project was the aerial mapping of as much of Antarctica as possible, particularly the coastline.

Assignments of ships to this Antarctic Expedition commenced on August 26, 1946, a total of 13 ships were chosen and they were assigned to one of four designated groups. The majority of the vessels began sailing for Antarctica in early December.

Over the next three months, nearly 5000 men participated in Operation Highjump. For the first time, modern icebreakers visited Antarctica and even a submarine was included in the task force to determine if it would be able to operate in Antarctic waters. Helicopters were also used for the first time in Antarctica.

The Central Group reached the Bay of Whales on January 15, 1947 and established Little America IV, complete with three compacted snow runways. The aircraft carrier Philippine Sea carried six R4-D transport aircraft (Navy version of the DC-3) and Admiral Byrd to the edge of the ice pack. The R4-Ds successfully took off from the flight deck of the Philippine Sea using JATO bottles attached under their wings and reached Little America six hours later. Admiral Byrd flew in the lead aircraft. Extensive aerial mapping was then conducted by the R4-Ds flying from Little America including a two aircraft flight to the South Pole on Feb 15-16.

Operations for the Eastern Group commenced in late December 1946 in the vicinity of Peter I island, north of the Bellingshausen Sea. Brownson took up her position as a weather station and flight operations commenced. The following day one of the Martin Mariner flying boats crashed on Thurston Island during a whiteout, killing three occupants of the aircraft. It was not until thirteen days later that the six survivors of the crash, including the commander of the Pine Island, were rescued.

Although the original mission statement declared that the operation would last for eight months, Admiral Byrd unexpectedly withdrew after only eight weeks. History books state that every objective for Operation Highjump had been met and Byrd saw no reason to remain any longer. However, rumors soon began circulating that there was more to the operation than was publicly admitted.

NAZI INVOLVEMENT WITH ANTARCTICA

It is now known that in the late 1930s Germany was involved in exploring certain areas of Antarctica. In 1938 the Germans undertook an expedition to Antarctica at a cost of some millions of Reichsmarks.

One odd piece of historical irony, in late 1938, Admiral Byrd visited Hamburg and was invited to participate in the 1938/1939 German expedition, but declined. That the expedition was military in nature seems beyond doubt, for the Nazis spared no effort to outfit the expedition as thoroughly as possible. As well, small teams of specially selected

Admiral Byrd's Secret Journey Beyond the Poles

biologists and other scientists accompanied the expedition to run laboratory experiments on board the specially outfitting seaplane carrier Schwabenland.

The Germans chose the region of Antarctica known as Queen Maud Land and in blatant disregard for international law, they overflew the area, dropping thousands of swastika flags, claiming it for Germany and renaming the region Neuschwabenland. The German pilots also extensively photographed the region, and allegedly found geothermal heated ice-free ponds in which grew various unknown species of algae.

They also discovered the southern tip of the fault line that runs from New Zealand, through Neuschwabenland, and up the Atlantic Ocean, the famous Atlantic "trench." The Germans concluded that such features might indicate the presence of geothermal heated rocky caverns that could be the perfect place for a hidden base in the inaccessible wilderness.

Historians still furiously debate the real reasons why Germany was so interested in Antarctica. Knowing what we know now about Hitler and his plans for world domination, it seems unlikely that the Germans were studying Antarctica for purely scientific reasons.

In the period before WWII the Germans wish to possess their own base in parts of Antarctica grew stronger. At this time the Antarctic was not safe due to international treaties and a pragmatic proof of Germany's claim by a single strike to the South Pole on the eve of the war seemed to be the best option.

Hitler was anxious for a foothold in the Antarctic and such a claim could be used very effectively for National Socialistic propaganda and a further demonstration of the new German superpower. On the other hand, provoking the Allies over the southern polar regions was something to be avoided as Germany was not completely prepared for the coming war.

So it was decided on the highest levels to keep further intrusions into Antarctica secret and after all the research was finished, deep underground construction teams came pouring into the renamed Neuschwabenland. They came on cargo ships, military transport ships, and submarines. As landing points, they used two of the three marked landing bays north-west of the Hlig-Hoffman Mountains scouted by earlier missions. Scientific teams were moved in to the area, including zoologists, botanists, agriculturists, mycologists, parasitologists, marine biologists, ornithologists, etc.

In 1940 the Nazis started to amass tractors, planes, sledges, gliders, and machinery at base camps within the continent. They scooped out an entire mountain, built a new refuge completely camouflaged. Nazi engineers had already begun construction of buildings that were to withstand temperatures to 60 degrees below zero.

The cargo ships coming from South Africa were protected by a host of U-Boats and military ships. This might explain the intense Nazi war efforts in North and South

Admiral Byrd's Secret Journey Beyond the Poles

Africa. Any ship that even came close to the shipping routes from South Africa to Antarctica was destroyed by German U-boats to protect the secret.

After all the materials were brought in, scientists and a highly specialized Nazi SS team called ULTRA arrived. Secret construction in Antarctica continued throughout the entire course of the war.

Just before the end of the war, two German provision U-boats, U-530 and U-977, were launched from a port on the Baltic Sea. Reportedly, they took with them members of the antigravity-disk research and development teams and the last of the most vital flying disc components. It is believed that much of this technology and hardware had been transported to the base during the course of the war.

This included the notes and drawings for the latest saucer or aerial disk designs, and designs for the gigantic underground complexes and living accommodations based on the remarkable underground factories of Nordhausen in the Harz Mountains. The two U-boats reached Neuschwabenland where they unloaded their precious cargo. When they arrived in Argentina several months later, their crews surrendered to the authorities. U.S. Navy officials immediately traveled down to Argentina and started intensive interrogations on the crew.

Captain Heinz Schäffer of the U-977 repeatedly denied to have transported any people or materials to Antarctica or South America. Although most of the crew were unwilling to tell what really happened, it is possible that these interrogations deliver important information about the location of a secret base.

During these interrogations, it was discovered that a fleet of almost twenty submarines sailed out from the Norwegian port of Bergen, between May 1, 1945 and the capitulation of the Third Reich, six days later. They joined another group of U-boats coming from the U.S. coasts (the U-530 and others) in Cape Verde, an Atlantic archipelago close to Africa. There, they were notified that the Flensburg Government, headed by Great Admiral Dõnitz after Hitler's death, and kept alive by the Western Allies until May 23 1945, had fallen.

Consequently, German commanders, who expected a new turn on international politics based on the outbreak of a conflict between the Soviet Union and the United States, became aware that they would have to go on by their own. Some Kriegmarine Officers decided to sink their U-boots, surrender to the enemy or go back to Europe. However, at least six U-boats, including the U-530 and the U-977, headed south to Antarctica carrying passengers, top-secret equipment and gold.

Top secret documents still classified by the U.S. and Great Britain acknowledge that the Nazi exodus to Antarctica had begun as early as September 1943 when high-ranking Nazi Officials realized that Germany was doomed to lose the war. The secret base in Antarctica was already completed by this time and plans were quickly drawn up to use Argentina as a staging country to assist the Nazi High Command in escaping

Admiral Byrd's Secret Journey Beyond the Poles

Europe. During the war, Argentina had remained officially neutral until early 1945, when economic pressure forced it to align with the Allies. However, the Argentine government was in intimate contact with Hitler's regime and the fascist Franco government in Spain. It is no surprise then that Argentina felt compelled to open its borders to the fleeing Nazis.

Argentine journalist Uki Goñi, in *The Real Odessa: Smuggling the Nazis to Peron's Argentina* (2002), says that about a dozen energetic ex-Nazis and Nazi collaborators from several nations, including a few wanted war criminals, working in concert with the Peron regime and sympathetic Catholic officials in both Europe and Argentina. Goñi makes a plausible case that the cabal, which was organized in Buenos Aires following Peron's election as Argentina's president in 1946, orchestrated the emigration of hundreds, perhaps thousands of Nazis and captive slave labor to the country in the late 1940s and early 1950s. In fact, the government of Argentina had issued at least 2,003 passports for high Nazi war criminals.

The old Nazis made frequent trips to Europe to troll for more fugitives; some war criminals had to be smuggled out, but in other cases countries were glad to unload their troublesome Nazi refugees. Visas and landing permits were handed out freely, the chief concern being that no communists or Jews be allowed in by mistake. How many ex-Nazis made it to Argentina is not known. Goñi says he identified 300 during six years of research, and it's easy to believe there were many more.

There are a few names available that tell of the secret Nazi plan for after the war. Martin Bormann was the highest-ranking SS officer to take refuge in South America, specifically in Chile and Argentina. Bormann joined the Nazi party in 1925, and by the end of WWII was Adolf Hitler's personal assistant.

Bormann became so powerful that he was appointed by Hitler to collect the financial donations made by the richest German businessmen to the Nazi party, and also to look after Hitler's private estate, such as the Berghof (Wolf's Lair) in Bavaria. In 1941, Bormann was appointed Chancellor of the Nazi Party, whereby all official matters and meetings with Hitler had to be previously approved by Bormann.

In 1945, as the Soviet troops advanced on the Berlin Bunker, Bormann witnessed Hitler and Eva Braun's wedding. After the ceremony Hitler ordered Bormann to escape and save his life to carry out a mysterious "final mission."

There are many versions as to how Bormann escaped from Berlin; some claim that he died others that he escaped. Bormann's final fate remained an enigma until 1996 when a passport was found in Chile with Bormann's photo but under the name of Ricardo Bauer. There is no doubt that the secret mission given to Bormann by Hitler was to eventually infiltrate and take over the Argentine government. Then, with the help and military muscle of the secret Neuschwabenland base, create the Fourth Reich.

Admiral Byrd's Secret Journey Beyond the Poles

DID HITLER ESCAPE TO ANTARCTICA?

It would be impossible to discuss the possibility of Nazi involvement with Antarctica without mentioning the widespread rumors that somehow Hitler escaped Berlin to live out the rest of his days in either Argentina or the secret Antarctic base. This rumor is an old one. It first surfaced in a book by Ladislao Szabo entitled ***Hitler Esta Vivo*** (***Hitler Is Alive***) back in 1947. Another book was written and published in 1969 by Michael X and was entitled: ***We Want You: Is Hitler Alive?***

Another journalist, Abel Basti, says, "Adolf Hitler lived in Patagonia, in southern Argentina, after fleeing Germany in 1945."

In an interview published on January 2, 2004 with the newspaper *Las Ultimas Noticias* of Santiago de Chile, Basti says that Hitler and his wife, Eva Braun, did not commit suicide - rather, they fled to Argentina's shores aboard a submarine and lived for years in the vicinity of San Carlos de Bariloche, a tourist site and ski haven about 1,350 kilometers (810 miles) southwest of Buenos Aires. In his book, ***Bariloche: Nazi Guia-Turistica***, published in 2004, Basti reproduces documents, affidavits, photographs and blueprints aimed at steering the reader to the sites that sheltered Hitler, Martin Bormann, Josef Mengele and Adolf Eichmann. When asked if his book challenges the official story of the Hitler/Braun suicide, Basti says that despite reports from the Soviets, the corpses of Hitler and his lover were never found, as is the case with other Nazis who allegedly committed suicide.

"The only 'official' story is the report made by General Zhukov (commander of the Soviet armies that occupied Berlin) to the Kremlin, stating that Hitler and several Nazi leaders had escaped, presumably to Spain or the Americas, and this is what Stalin advised the U.S. government, he retorted."

Basti's book includes a photo of the Incalco Ranch (In the language of the indigenous Nahuel people of Argentina, Incalco means near the water), located in Villa la Angostura on the shores of Lago Nahuel Huapi (lake), 80 kilometers (50 miles) north of Bariloche. This was the refuge chosen by Argentinean Nazis to hide Hitler and Eva Braun.

"This residence, set amidst a pine forest and which can only be reached by boat or hydroplane, belonged to Argentinean businessman Jorge Antonio, one of the most trusted aides of two-time president Juan Domingo Peron."

Basti makes mention of Rudolph Fraude, son of Ludwig Fraude, the German millionaire, as a key player, in his capacity as Peron's secretary, in placing former Nazis in Argentina, among them Adolf Eichmann, who was captured in 1960 outside Buenos Aires by Israeli commandos. He was executed two years later in Israel.

The book's author, having been involved in several Nazi-related investigations with European television networks, claims that Hitler also lived at Hacienda San

Admiral Byrd's Secret Journey Beyond the Poles

Ramon, 10 kilometers (6 miles) east of Bariloche, which belonged at the time to the (German) principality of Schaumberg-Lippe.

"There is numerous and reliable evidence that Nazis fled to Argentina, with the arrival of Nazi U-boats in Patagonia," Basti noted, recalling the vital assistance offered by Peron's government at the time to admit the Führer's henchmen into that country.

There are eyewitness accounts from qualified people who were with Hitler in Argentina and who agree with FBI, British Intelligence, and Argentinean Navy documents discussing the presence of Nazi subs in the South Atlantic in July and August 1945. Furthermore, there is additional information that contradicts the alleged suicide of Hitler. The first official reports talk of an escape. In other words, when the Red Army entered the bunker, Stalin asked for a confirmation of Hitler's death and the general in charge says he couldn't because there was no body.

Research shows that there were a number of surface and submersible ships evacuating the Nazi high command from Europe. They first traveled to South America and many afterwards, including possibly Hitler, continued on to Antarctica. If the rumors of a secret Nazi base were only the ravings of conspiracy madmen, why did so many Nazi submarines make the perilous journey to the South Pole?

So is there any truth to these rumors that Hitler may have escaped Berlin to live out the rest of his life either in Argentina or Neuschwabenland? In his well-documented ***The Hitler Survival Myth*** (1981), Donald McKale identifies the earliest source of the myth of Hitler's escape to the unexpected surrender of a German submarine in early July 1945 at Mar del Plata, Argentina.

Several Buenos Aires newspapers, in defiance of Argentine Navy statements, said that rubber boats had been seen landing from it and other submarines spotted in the area. One paper, *Critica*, carried on July 17, 1945 the report that Hitler and Eva Braun had been taken to Antarctica aboard the U-530. The article also mentioned the 1938-39 Antarctic expedition, as a result of which a "new Berchtesgaden" was "likely to have been built."

This report received wide distribution with *Le Monde*, the *New York Times* and the *Chicago Times* reporting on July 18 that Hitler and Braun had survived and had secretly slipped away to Antarctica. These articles are probably the first reports to publicly reveal the secret Neuschwabenland Nazi base.

After the United States military interrogated the captains and crew of the U-530 and U-977, concern began to grow in Washington that the Nazi threat was not over. Secret channels in Great Britain were also abuzz with stories of a new Nazi stronghold in Antarctica. With the ever-growing threat of the Soviet Union, the Western Powers did not have the military resources to take on another Nazi front in the icy wastes of Antarctica. Even more frightening, there were rumors that the Nazis were not alone on the vast, frozen southern continent.

Admiral Byrd's Secret Journey Beyond the Poles

BRITAIN'S SECRET WAR IN ANTARCTICA

James Robert, in his article *Britain's Secret War in Antarctica*, published in the August - September 2005 issue of *Nexus* magazine, states that at the end of World War II, Britain sent a covert mission to investigate anomalous activities near its secret base at Maudheim in eastern Antarctica and to seek out and destroy a subterranean Nazi haven.

Roberts states that his information came from the last survivor of the British Neuschwabenland campaign who said that their mission in 1945 was an evasive action because Britain was well aware of U.S. and USSR intentions in mounting their own expeditions, and Britain did not want to risk the chance that the U.S. or the USSR would discover the base and gain further Nazi technology.

Furthermore, the British Special Forces were told that radio communications with the secret Maudheim base had been lost in July, 1945 after strange claims over the radio about "Polar Men, ancient tunnels and Nazis." The last broadcast was a panicked voice that screamed: "...the Polar Men have found us!" before contact was lost.

Upon arriving in Antarctica, the Special Forces found one survivor who told of an expedition to a "dry valley" where a mysterious tunnel was discovered. Every one of the thirty personnel at the Maudheim base was ordered to investigate and, if possible, find out exactly where the tunnel led. They followed the tunnel for miles, and eventually they came to a vast underground cavern that was abnormally warm; some of the scientists believed that it was warmed geothermally.

In the huge cavern were underground lakes; however, the mystery deepened, as the cavern was lit artificially. The cavern proved so extensive that they had to split up, and that was when the real discoveries were made.

The Nazis had constructed a huge base into the caverns and had even built docks for U-boats, and one was identified supposedly. Still, the deeper they traveled, the more strange visions they were greeted with. The survivor reported that "hangars for strange planes and extensive excavations" had been documented.

However, their presence had not gone unnoticed: the two survivors at the Maudheim base witnessed their comrades' get captured and executed one by one. After witnessing only six of the executions, they fled to the tunnel, lest they be caught, with the aim to block up the tunnel—though "it was too late; the Polar Men were coming," claimed the survivor.

With enemy forces not far behind, they had no choice but to try to get back to the base so that they could inform and warn their superiors about what they had uncovered. They managed to get back to the base, but, with winter approaching and little chance of rescue, they believed it was their duty to make sure the secret Nazi base was reported; and so they split up, each taking a wireless and waiting in separate bunkers.

Admiral Byrd's Secret Journey Beyond the Poles

One of the survivors tempted one of the Polar Men into the bunker in the hope that they'd believe only one had survived. The plan worked, but he was killed in the process and the radio destroyed.

Unfortunately, the brave soul in Bunker One had the only fully operational wireless radio, which was destroyed in the fracas. The other survivor had no option but to sit, wait and try to avoid going stir crazy.

The mystery of who or what the Polar Men were was explained, not satisfactorily, but explained nonetheless as a product of Nazi science; and the enigma of how the Nazis were getting power was also explained, albeit not in scientific terms. The power that the Nazis were utilizing was by volcanic activity, which gave them heat for steam and also helped produce electricity, but the Nazis had also mastered an unknown energy source.

The British would eventually return to the tunnel and witness for themselves the secret Nazi Base which they allegedly destroyed with planted explosives. But according to the rumors that continue to fly around the United States Operation Highjump, the Nazi presence in Antarctica was still a force to be reckoned with in 1947.

This brings us back once again to the allegations in *The Missing Diary of Admiral Byrd* that Byrd, while on a flight over the North Pole (or South Pole if history is correct), was intercepted by strange flying discs bearing Swastikas and taken to a strange city supposedly inside the inner Earth. The book states that Byrd's experience in 1947 occurred over the Arctic, but we know that at that time Admiral Byrd was involved with Operation Highjump in the Antarctic. Could it be that *The Missing Diary of Admiral Byrd* is an attempt by someone to circumnavigate the news blackout that has been created around Operation Highjump?

Might this book be part of a campaign to reveal the truth on what really happened in February 1947? A truth that so rattled the Admiral that he told the Chilean newspaper *El Mercurio* that it was "imperative for the United States to initiate immediate defense measures against hostile regions?" Furthermore, Byrd stated that he "didn't want to frighten anyone unduly but that it was a bitter reality that in case of a new war the continental United States would be attacked by flying objects which could fly from pole to pole at incredible speeds."

However, what sort of flying objects would be operating out of the Antarctic with the ability to intercept modern aircraft and threaten the mightiest superpowers on the planet?

Above: U-Boat 530
Below: U-Boat 977
Were these submarines part of a secret flotilla to take Nazi scientists and technology to Antarctica?

CHAPTER SIX
Nazi Flying Saucers – Technology From the Hollow Earth?

In 1947, Admiral Richard E. Byrd led 4,000 military troops from the U.S. in what was said to be a scientific expedition of Antarctica. Codenamed Operation Highjump, this so-called scientific expedition was actually an invasion of Antarctica to try and root out a suspected Nazi base hidden in the Queen Maud region that the Germans had renamed Neuschwabenland.

Intelligence collected by both the Allies and the Soviet Union indicated that the German High Command had sent manpower, machinery and materials to Antarctica to construct a secret base as a "last option" to keep the Third Reich going after the inevitable fall of Berlin. Those closest to Hitler knew that his reign would soon end disastrously, but many high ranking officers still felt that the Third Reich could continue under the right leadership.

Secret overtures had been made to the Allies, especially Great Britain, as early as 1941 when Deputy Führer Rudolf Hess flew to Scotland to conduct a secret meeting to end the war with Great Britain. Unfortunately, Hess's secret meeting was discovered and his mission was sabotaged.

Because of this, Nazi leaders realized that a war with the West that also included the Soviet Union would spell doom for the Third Reich. It was decided that in order to preserve the true essence of the Third Reich, there had to be safe havens created so that both people and technology could be secreted away. One such technological development was the German flying disc, whose creation was so shocking that the U.S. continues to this day to deny its existence.

THE DEVELOPMENT OF THE FLYING SAUCER

In the early 1900's there were a variety of secret/occult societies in Germany, the main ones being, The Bavarian Illuminati, The Freemasons, the Rosicrucians, The Thule Society and The Vril Society. Each of these five societies, although based in secrecy and mysticism, had its role and function. Of these five, two were especially noted for their occult connections, The Vril Society and its purely German offshoot The Thule Society.

The Thule Society was formed in 1917. Located in Munich, it was a melting pot of many orders. In 1921 Hitler was engaged as an orator and, inspired by the beliefs of the Thule Society, his plan for a thousand year Reich was born.

Admiral Byrd's Secret Journey Beyond the Poles

Rear Admiral Richard Byrd revisits his old hut at the site of Little America II. He is smoking 12-year old tobacco in a 12-year old corncob pipe left at the camp in 1935. This photo was taken in 1947 during Operation Highjump.

Admiral Byrd's Secret Journey Beyond the Poles

The Vril Society, formed in 1919, was an offshoot of the Thule Society. This group included mediums and experts on ancient philosophies and scripts, particularly those of the Sumerians and Babylonians. There were also two scientists who were well-versed in alternative energies. It was their aim to communicate with luminaries from the past and even to travel in time.

The chief architect of the Thule Society was Baron Rudolf von Sebottendorff, sometimes referred to as Rudolf Glauer. Sebottendorff/Glauer possessed a wide knowledge of Islamic Mysticism in all its aspects, encompassing the Dervish sects and particularly the cult of Sufism, which differs markedly from mainstream Islamic teaching.

In 1917, four people met in a cafe in Vienna. There was one woman and three men. The woman, Maria Orsitsch, was a spiritual medium who believed she was receiving information from Aryan aliens living on a planet in the Aldebaran star system in the Taurus Constellation, 64 light years away.

They met under a veil of mystery and secrecy. They discussed secret revelations, the coming of the new age, the sphere of destiny, the magical violet black stone, and making contact with ancient peoples and distant worlds. The Vril emblem was the "Black Sun" - a secret philosophy thousand of years old provided the foundation on which the occult practitioners of the Third Reich would later build. The Black Sun symbol can be found in many Babylonian and Assyrian places of worship. They depicted the Black Sun - the godhead's inner light in the form of a cross. This was not much different from the German's Knight's Cross.

The Vril Force or Vril Energy was said to be derived from the Black Sun, a big ball of "Prima Materia" which supposedly exists in the center of the Earth, giving light to the Vril-ya and putting out radiation in the form of Vril. The Vril Society believed that Aryans were the actual biological ancestors of the Black Sun.

With important information supposedly channeled from the extraterrestrials, the Vril society built the Vril Machine; a saucer-shaped machine that was an interdimensional or time travel machine. This craft was called the Jenseitsflugmaschine, or "Other World Flight Machine." The Thule and Vril societies used their members in the German business community to raise funds for the construction of this machine under the code letters J-F-M. By 1922, parts for the machine began arriving independently from various industrial sources paid in full by the Thule and Vril.

The machine itself was in disc form with three inner disc plates inside its plate-like hull and a cylindrical power unit running through the center of all three plates. Once activated, the cylindrical power unit, which consisted of an electric starter motor and high power generator, started the upper and lower disc plates equipped with electromagnets spinning in opposite directions to create strong rotating electromagnetic fields that were increasingly field-intensified.

Admiral Byrd's Secret Journey Beyond the Poles

The intensity of the electromagnetic fields were manipulated to create frequency field oscillations that increased up to a point where an inter-dimensional oscillation occurred - a "channel" which opened a "gateway" or portal to another universal system or world. The occultists called this a "white hole" that theoretically would connect the Jenseitsflugmaschine to Aldebaran's corresponding frequency oscillations and navigate the machine through to that system to meet up with the Sumerian Fleet (an alien fleet awaiting them).

The sole purpose of this machine was to reach Aldebaran and make contact directly with those Aryan aliens that had supplied the technical information through psychic revelation. Unlike an imploding black hole that uses its destructive gravitic force to theoretically punch a hole through the fabric of space/time, the occultists believed in non-destructive manipulation of gravity through high-intensity field oscillations to gradually open a small channel in space/time just wide enough to pass the Jenseitsflugmaschine through.

Two years of flight research was performed with the Jenseitsflugmaschine until 1924 when the machine was hurriedly dismantled and moved to Augsburg where it eventually was placed in storage at Messerschmitt's facility. From there, additional research led to the development of a next generation of flying discs that the Nazis hoped would stop the Allied advance upon Germany.

A number of different concepts were built and tested. Flugkapitän Rudolf Schriever came up with the idea of a "Flugkreisel" (Flight Gyro) that was powered by developing turbojet technology. Viktor Schauberger, an Austrian forester who observed the effects of nature-especially of water, developed a revolutionary vortex motor in 1940 called the Repulsin(e), roughly translated as "Repulsor." The first model, the Repulsin A was a colloidal disc motor that utilized air and water contained in a copper casing to produce a mini-tornado, or vortex, inside the machine that caused levitation at some point.

BMW started development of its own versions of the new "disc-fan" technology called the Flügelrad that was powered by two BMW 003 jet engines located in the lower body side-by-side. The Flügelrad lay-out was of a central body housing that could hold two pilots covered by a hemispheric dome surrounded by a disc blade rotor.

During the early 1940's Dr. Richard Miethe produced many different Flugscheiben (Flight Disc) designs for the SS in a concentrated effort to improve or replace Rudolf Schriever's failing disc-fan Flugkreisel prototype. He was not alone as Schriever's original design was handed over to Dr. Miethe, Klaus Habermohl, Dr. Giuseppe Belluzzo, and six other unnamed engineers - all producing several radical designs based on the emerging engine technologies.

But perhaps the most unorthodox propulsion system yet incorporated into one of Miethe's designs was based on the work of Austrian physicist Dr. Karl Nowak which

Admiral Byrd's Secret Journey Beyond the Poles

involved oxygen and nitrogen. The power plant involved burned nothing but air. The scientists achieved this by building a reciprocating engine which used atmospheric oxygen to oxidize atmospheric nitrogen.

Very intense electrical voltage sparks were needed to produce temperatures near 50,000 degrees within the combustion chamber - with the same natural effect as lightning. Only the Air engine also injected super-cold helium directly into the combustion chamber for the dual purpose of cooling the chamber and also causing a tremendous expansion during heating, thus aiding in the driving force of the engine itself.

This design which Bruno Schwenteit patented postwar was claimed to be the Miethe-Schriever disc so often labeled the mystery V-7. Schwenteit also claimed the disc was actually constructed during World War II.

Another version of this extremely convoluted story says that Dr. Miethe found the solution when word came of Schauberger's completion of the Repulsin B model discoid motor in 1943 and its radical vortex propulsion system that could be reasonably enlarged into a manned disc of incredible power.

Work proceeded right away and by April 1944 the Miethe craft constructed in Breslau took off for flight tests over the Baltic. It was reported to Hitler on April 17, 1944 by the SS that the Miethe disc had successfully flown.

Viktor Schauberger stated in the 1950's that he worked at the Mauthausen concentration camp directing technically oriented prisoners and German scientists in the successful construction of a saucer-shaped aircraft: "The 'flying saucer' which was flight-tested on the 19th February 1945 near Prague and which attained a height of 15,000 meters in three minutes and a horizontal speed of 2,200 km/hours (1,366mph!), was constructed according to a Model 1 built at Mauthausen concentration camp in collaboration with the first-class stress-analyst and propulsion engineers assigned to me there."

Schriever's original Flugkreisel was reported to have flown in February 1945 where it attained a top speed of 1,300 mph and a climb to 45,000 ft. in two minutes. BMW's Flügelrads by comparison could barely get off the ground, were highly unstable, and made frequent "hard" landings. Only one Flügelrad II V-2 (or V-3) finally achieved powered level flight in April 1945 just before all the Flügelrads and Schriever's Flugkreisel were destroyed in the Russian advance.

However, were these extraordinary aircraft actually destroyed, or were they taken apart and shipped to a safe location out of the reach of the approaching Allied forces? This is not an outrageous claim – it is a well-known fact that the Nazis were planning a post Word War II return.

A September 14, 2000 news release by Reuters states that according to a newly declassified U.S. intelligence document, Nazi leaders met top German industrialists to plan a secret post-war international network to restore them to power when they realized that they were losing the war in 1944.

The document, which appears to confirm a meeting historians have long argued about, says an SS general and a representative of the German armaments ministry told such companies as Krupp and Roehling that they must be prepared to finance the Nazi party after the war when it went underground. They were also told, "Existing financial reserves in foreign countries must be placed at the disposal of the party so that a strong German empire can be created after the defeat."

The document, detailing an August 1944 meeting, was obtained from the World Jewish Congress, which has been working with the Senate Banking Committee and the Holocaust Museum to determine what happened to looted Jewish money and property in the Second World War.

As a result of the probe, thousands of documents from "Operation Safehaven" were made public. The operation was a U.S. intelligence effort to track how the German government used Swiss banks during the war to hide looted Jewish assets. The three-page document, released by the National Archives, was sent from Supreme Headquarters of the Allied Expeditionary Force to the U.S. secretary of state in November 1944. It described a secret meeting at the Maison Rouge (the Red House Hotel) in Strasbourg, occupied France, on August 10, 1944.

The source for the report was an agent who attended and "had worked for the French on German problems since 1916." Jeffrey Bale, a Columbia University expert on clandestine Nazi networks, said historians have debated whether such a meeting could have taken place because it came a month after the attempt on Adolf Hitler's life, which had led to a crackdown on discussions of a possible German military defeat. Bale said the Red House meeting was mentioned in Nazi hunter Simon Wiesenthal's 1967 book **The Murderers Among Us** and again in a 1978 book by French Communist Victor Alexandrov, **The SS Mafia**.

A U.S. Treasury Department analysis in 1946 reported that the Germans had transferred $500 million out of the country before the war's end to countries such as Spain, Switzerland, Lichtenstein, Portugal, Argentina and Turkey where it was used to buy hundreds of companies. "As soon as the (Nazi) party becomes strong enough tore-establish its control over Germany, the industrialists will be paid for their efforts and cooperation by concessions and orders," the intelligence document said. The meeting was presided over by a "Dr Scheid," described as an SS Obergruppenf ührer (general) and director of Hermsdorff & Schonburg Company. Attending were representatives of seven German companies including Krupp, Roehling, Messerschmidt, and Volkswagenwerk and officials of the ministries of armaments and the navy.

The industrialists were from companies with extensive interests in France and Scheid is quoted as saying the battle of France was lost and "from now...German

Admiral Byrd's Secret Journey Beyond the Poles

industry must realize that the war cannot be won and it must take steps in preparation for a post-war commercial campaign." He said

German industry must make contacts and alliances with foreign firms and lay the groundwork for borrowing considerable sums in foreign countries. He cited the Krupp Company's sharing of patents with U.S. companies so that they would have to work with Krupp. A representative of the armaments ministry then presided over a smaller second meeting with Scheid and representatives of Krupp and Roehling, who were told the war was lost and would continue only until the unity of Germany was guaranteed. He said they must prepare themselves to finance the Nazi party when it went underground.

The intelligence report added that the meetings signaled a new Nazi policy whereby industrialists with government assistance will export as much of their capital as possible. Sybil Milton, senior historian at Washington's Holocaust Museum, said it has long been known that the Nazis planned to do something after the war and the document's importance may be in pointing researchers in a direction where they could determine what had been done.

Researchers long before the release of this document had already been following the tracks left by the fleeing Nazis. These tracks led all across the globe, into the United States, South America and into Antarctica. The United States Government was well aware that a large group of Nazis had established themselves in Antarctica. The whole idea of Operation Highjump was to root out this "last stronghold" of Nazi elites. But, the U.S. had no idea that the Nazis were not totally helpless and had at their disposal technology that allowed them to defend themselves from the attacking U.S. forces.

Ray Palmer in an editorial for *Search Magazine* wrote that secret Nazi documents seized by Allied forces told of spiritual mediums for the Vril society who had established contact with highly evolved beings who lived in the hollow Earth. These "inner Earth" people revealed that in the southern polar regions, there was a secret underground entrance that led to one of their great cities.

Palmer continued that sources in Argentina confirmed this revelation and added further details stating that German flying disc technology had been greatly improved with the help from the inner Earth race. Originally, the Flugkreisel relied upon jets to provide thrust, now they were more akin to the original Vril Jenseitsflugmaschine that had been locked away before the war because the technology was so completely unknown and alien.

With this new development, the Neuschwabenland base caught Operation Highjump completely off guard. Sources differ on what was the actual outcome. Some say that Highjump suffered disastrous losses in both equipment and personnel. But, if we go back and look more closely at the book *The Missing Diary of Admiral Byrd*, we have some clues on what may have actually occurred.

Admiral Byrd's Secret Journey Beyond the Poles

ADMIRAL BYRDS MYSTERIOUS ENCOUNTER

In *The Missing Diary of Admiral Byrd*, Byrd is allegedly making a flight over the North Pole in February 1947 when actually he was in Antarctica at this time overseeing Operation Highjump. It has been assumed that the story of Byrd making a North Pole journey in 1947 is either a mistake based on his earlier 1927 flight, or a flat-out hoax. But, looking at some details in The Missing Diary of Admiral Byrd, it seems likely that the book is actually revealing an unexpected encounter with Byrd and Nazi flying discs over their secret Antarctic base; an encounter that was supposed to be kept top secret.

Admiral Byrd's teams of six R4-D's (DC-3's) were fitted with cameras and each plane was trailing a magnetometer, mapping and recording magnetic data. Magnetometers show anomalies in the Earth's magnetism, i.e. if there is a hollow place under the surface ice or ground, it would show up on the meter.

On the last of many mapping flights where all six planes went out, each on certain pre-ordained paths to film and measure with magnetometers, Admiral Byrd's plane returned three hours late. It was stated that they had lost an engine and had to limp back to base. Shortly thereafter, Operation Highjump was prematurely ended and the expedition quickly left the area.

This probably was the event written about in *The Missing Diary of Admiral Byrd* – just replace North Pole for South Pole and a picture begins to emerge of Admiral Byrd on a photographic mission in an attempt to gain important strategic information about the Nazi Neuschwabenland base. During this secret mission, Byrd's plane was intercepted by two flying saucers and forced to land.

In the book, at 1130 hours – it says that "Countryside below is more level and normal (if I may use that word). Ahead we spot what seems to be a city!!!! This is impossible! Aircraft seems light and oddly buoyant. The controls refuse to respond!! My GOD!!! Off our port and starboard wings are a strange type of aircraft. They are closing rapidly alongside! They are disc-shaped and have a radiant quality to them. They are close enough now to see the markings on them. It is a type of Swastika!!! This is fantastic. Where are we! What has happened? I tug at the controls again. They will not respond!!!! We are caught in an invisible vice grip of some type!"

Byrd notes that he can see Swastikas on the flying discs. This is a significant point considering that Byrd was in Antarctica looking for a hidden Nazi base. The tall-blond pilots of the discs speak to Byrd in what he describes as a Nordic or Germanic accent, and they call their discs "Flugelrads," which according to some, is an actual German word meaning "wing-wheels."

In the book, Byrd is taken for an audience with "the Master" where he is told that the inner world civilization has been closely watching the surface world with growing

Admiral Byrd's Secret Journey Beyond the Poles

interest, especially after the atomic bomb explosions in Japan. Finally, at the end as Byrd and his radioman are allowed to leave, his hosts bid them Auf Wiedersehen. Hardly a farewell one would expect from a highly advanced underground civilization who has kept their distance from the primitive surface world. But, it is a fitting farewell from a secret group of Nazis who are intent to let the rest of the world know that the Third Reich may have been defeated, but the Fourth Reich is ready and able to defend itself from attack.

As for the rest of the story, the lush, green valleys, the mammoths; these could all be red herrings or disinformation to allow the story to get out to the public a little bit at a time. Or it could all be true. The Germans have a secret base in Antarctica with the help of the inner Earth residents who come and go through a gigantic hole located somewhere on the frozen continent.

Whatever the case, Admiral Byrd did have some sort of earth-shaking experience that led him to withdraw his forces early and to make statements to the press that the polar regions were somehow dangerous to the rest of the planet. When Byrd returned to the States, he was hospitalized and was not allowed to hold any more press conferences. *The Missing Diary of Admiral Byrd* and other sources state that the U.S. government warned Byrd about talking about what really happened to him in Antarctica.

A few months later, starting in June of 1947, the United States saw its skies invaded by unknown flying craft. These machines were dubbed "flying saucers" by the press and speculation quickly arose that the planet was being visited by beings from other planets.

Even more bizarre, in July 1947, something crashed in the desert near the town of Roswell, New Mexico. At that time the Roswell Army Airfield was the home of the 509th Bomb Group which was the only nuclear air group in the world. Could it be that the Nazis from their secret Antarctic base were letting the world know that they were able to fly with impunity through the airspace of the mightiest country in the world, and no one could do anything to prevent them from doing so?

Even though the civilian press contemplated that the UFO "invasion" might be extraterrestrials from outer space, officials at the Pentagon were more afraid that the flying discs had a more Earthly origin. Not only were they afraid of the possibility that Admiral Byrd's reports of a superior German force in Antarctica were correct, they also feared that the Soviet Union had come into possession of captured Nazi disc technology.

This was a very real fear as the Allied forces had not only managed to get their hands on Nazi scientists who had worked on the flying discs, but they had also managed to capture at least one and probably more intact Nazi-developed flying discs. These discs were carefully researched and back-engineered by top scientists from the U.S.,

Admiral Byrd's Secret Journey Beyond the Poles

along with help from German scientists brought over as part of the secret Operation Paperclip.

The Pentagon was well aware that Richard Miethe's A-7 flying top had been seized by the Russians at the end of the war, but fortunately, Herr Miethe had managed to escape the Soviet army and resettled in the United States. With the help of the government he found employment with the Canadian A.V. Roe Company, home of the star-crossed "Avro Car" saucer design under the Air Force "Silver Bug" VTOL umbrella program. But even without the help from Miethe, the U.S. military worried that the Soviets had been able to construct their own secret flying disc, and were now using them to fly over sensitive military areas.

This fear was somewhat diminished by the UFO crashes near Roswell in 1947 and Aztec, NM in 1948. The popular opinion was that inside these crashed UFOs were found the bodies of extraterrestrial beings. However, this seems to be recent disinformation to cover up the real fact that these UFOs were not being flown by little gray men from outer space; nor were they being piloted by Soviet communists. Instead, they were clearly identified as being former Nazi Air Force pilots that had went missing at the end of the war.

The United States was now faced with a worrisome dilemma. Admiral Byrd had returned from Operation Highjump with his tale of a secret Nazi base located in Antarctica. He had informed his superiors that this base might also be receiving assistance from some unknown race that originated from within the hollow Earth.

Pentagon officials could deal with the fact that some Nazis had managed to escape to the South Pole. But the idea that these pilots were also flying high-technology, disc-shaped aircraft **and** were being helped by creatures of the inner world, this was more than the Generals could bear. Admiral Byrd was ordered to stop talking about his encounter and was warned that his career in the military was in jeopardy if he decided to ignore these orders.

This idea was also suggested by the late Col. Philip J. Corso in his book ***The Day After Roswell.***

"Worse, the fact that this craft and other flying saucers had been surveilling our defensive installations and even seemed to evidence a technology we'd seen evidenced by the Nazis caused the military to assume these flying saucers had hostile intentions and might have even interfered in human events during the war."

"At the very least, Twining had suggested, the crescent-shaped craft looked so uncomfortably like the German Horten wings our flyers had seen at the end of the war that he had to suspect the Germans had bumped into something we didn't know about. And his conversations with Wernher von Braun and Willy Ley at Alamogordo in the days after the crash confirmed this. They didn't want to be thought of as verrukt but intimated that there was a deeper story about what the Germans had engineered."

Admiral Byrd's Secret Journey Beyond the Poles

From 1947 on, the skies of planet Earth seemed to be filled with the mysterious flying saucers. Washington DC even experienced an "air invasion" on July 19 and 26, 1952. Buzzing over the White House, the Capitol building, and the Pentagon, the unknown objects seemed to be brazenly defying the U.S military. Washington National Airport and Andrews Air Force Base picked up a number of UFOs on their radar screens traveling at about 100 M.P.H. but with the ability to accelerate to the unbelievable speed of 7,200 M.P.H.

Andrews Air Force Base notified the U.S. Air Force Air Defense Command. A couple of F-94 night fighters were ordered to the skies, but runway repairs held their mission up for several hours.

By the time they were airborne, the mysterious objects were gone. The fighters returned home, but soon the objects again showed up on the radar screens. For the next several hours, the fighters chased the illusive targets, but to no avail.

They were able to sight the UFOs, but lights of the unknown objects would darken as they were approached. Constant communication was kept with ground radar, and as the pilots lost sight of the UFOs, they also disappeared from ground radar. The UFOs were also separately witnessed by the crew of a B-29, and other commercial flights.

After a quiet week, the objects reappeared on July 26. After multiple radar operators confirmed the objects, the F-94s again began their search for the enigmatic lights over Washington. The results of their pursuit were identical to the week before. They could see the lights, but when they drew near, the lights would black out.

After their fruitless journey, the planes returned home, only to hear that the objects again were being tracked by radar. One of the pilots stated his fear and frustration by air to ground radio. "They've surrounded my plane, what should I do?" The phenomenal sights would bring about an Air Force press conference on July 29, with Major General John A. Samford in charge.

The official explanation was "temperature inversions," which supposedly caused ground lights to bounce off of clouds, giving the appearance of lighted craft in the skies. This explanation was scoffed at by ufologists who knew that it just did not explain what was seen by pilots and radar operators. Even *Project Bluebook* would also dismiss the temperature inversion explanation, as it later labeled the Washington sightings as "unknown."

The Washington DC sightings are a solid case of UFO activity. Literally hundreds of eyewitnesses saw the objects, and photographed them. Many of these were Air Force personnel, considered as reliable. Many of them made comment of the sightings, one was a Sergeant Harrison: "I saw the...light moving from the Northeast toward the range station. These lights did not have the characteristics of shooting stars. There were no trails and seemed to go out rather than disappear, and traveled faster than any shooting star I have ever seen."

Admiral Byrd's Secret Journey Beyond the Poles

This event may have been the pivotal point for the U.S. government to finally sit up and take notice of the Nazi UFO threat. It has been suggested that by this time communications and even diplomatic overtures had been conducted between the U.S. and Base 211, as the Antarctic location had become known. However, the constant flyovers of UFOs over U.S. territory was more than likely considered unacceptable by the government and a decision to finally do something about the problem had to be made.

According to the book *Reich of the Black Sun* by Joseph P. Farrell, Admiral Byrd and the United States returned to Antarctica, this time with nuclear force. Once again it was announced to the press that this was an "international cooperative effort," the International Geophysical Year of 1957- 1958. The use of military force, including atomic weapons, was covered by the story that the U.S. and USSR, in a rare moment of nuclear cooperation during the height of the Cold War, were interested in seeing how much of the continent could be "recovered" for use by warming it with nuclear explosions. Accordingly, it would be necessary to explode a few small nuclear devices above the continent to warm and melt the ice as a proof of concept.

Three nuclear bombs were detonated above Base 211; one on August 27, 1958, one on August 30, 1958, and a third on September 6, 1958. It is thought that the airbursts were intended to knock out German electronic equipment by the strong electromagnetic pulse (EMP) that occurs during a nuclear detonation.

THE MYSTERY CONTINUES

So what happened to Nazi Base 211? There is little information from this point on to either confirm or deny its continuation. With the Geophysical Year expedition of 1958's atomic detonations, the alleged German base on the Antarctic continent fades from attention. Allegedly, the Germans themselves gradually evacuated Base 211 during the interim period from Byrd's 1947 expedition to the final coup de grace for more favorable climes in South America. There are even stories that suggest the Germans moved completely underground through the South Polar opening into the inner world.

In his book *Adolf Hitler and the Secrets of the Holy Lance*, Howard A. Buechner details how the Holy Lance of Jesus was secretly taken to Base 211 in 1945. It is well known that Hitler and the inner core of the SS had a strong interest and belief in the occult and made every effort to collect both information and artifacts that held mystical significance.

The SS had actively searched for information that would lead them to the city of Agharta, the mystical realm of enlightened beings who lived inside the hollow Earth. Base 211 had been established in the Antarctic because this was supposedly the closest point on the surface world to the secret entrance to Agharta.

Admiral Byrd's Secret Journey Beyond the Poles

In 1979, an expedition to Antarctica was undertaken to find Base 211 and recover the Holy Lance. Jerry E. Smith, in his article *The Final Secret of the Holy Lance*, says that the expedition located and removed steel plates placed over the entrance to the Lance's hiding place and found a steel lined tunnel leading into the mountain.

Quoting from the expedition's log we read: "Our lights penetrate the steel tunnel which extends for approximately ten meters. When we arrive at the end of the tunnel, we find ourselves in a huge cavernous area. It seems warm. As we search the cavern with our lights, we notice frozen pillars of ice in strange and grotesque shapes. We penetrate into the cavern the distance of about 300 meters. It is at this point that we came to a smaller cavern which turned towards the right and ended in a room approximately 80 meters in width and ten meters in height. It is here that the Reich treasures are hidden.

"At this point stands a small obelisk about a meter in height which marks the spot. There is an inscription which reads as follows: "There are truly more things in heaven and 'in' earth than man has dreamt (Beyond this point is AGHARTA) Haushofer, 1943."

In the now deserted base, the expedition finds the Holy Lance and brings it back to Germany. However, the reason this story is being repeated for this book is that by 1979 the secret Nazi base has been abandoned. Considering that UFOs did not disappear after 1958, it is not unreasonable to believe that the Fourth Reich is still hiding somewhere, continuing its forays through the skies of the planet.

Does this mean that ALL unidentified flying objects are of Nazi origin? Absolutely not; the UFO phenomenon seems to actually be a number of different types of phenomena, all superficially resembling each other. UFOs could also be interplanetary spaceships; or time machines; or interdimensional; or paranormal; or from the hollow Earth; or all of the above.

Nazi flying discs are just one possible explanation for UFOs. Probably there is an aerodynamic reason why the disc-shape is so predominate in UFO sightings. This could explain why unidentified flying objects come from a number of different sources; the disc shape is what works best for the technology being used; be it antigravity, or whatever. The shape of the craft is the key, not the origin.

The story of Admiral Byrd's alleged adventure into the hollow Earth is convoluted and bizarre. Skeptics would like to dismiss it completely because the entire concept of the hollow Earth flies in the face of excepted geological theory. Proponents see Byrd's tale as proof positive of the reality of the inner world.

The truth, more than likely, lies somewhere in-between. The occult SS certainly believed in the hollow Earth. The SS, with assistance from the Vril and Thule societies, mounted a number of expeditions to places such as Tibet in order to gain insight on how best to discover tunnels to the inner world, or even how to approach the polar openings

Admiral Byrd's Secret Journey Beyond the Poles

to circumnavigate the gravitational anomalies that usually prevent those on the surface from entering the world below.

This may be why the Nazis chose Antarctica to establish their secret Base 211; because they were instructed to do so by a subterranean race that was speaking through Vril society mediums. With the help of this inner world race, the Germans were able to take their flying discs, do away with the primitive jets and rockets that were first used to fly them and utilize a form of antigravity propulsion that was years ahead of the science of the day.

The question remains whether or not Antarctic Base 211 is still active. There is no conclusive evidence that the Nazis still inhabit Antarctica. Jerry Smith notes that writer Wilhelm Landig, in novel form, described secret post-war German bases in Antarctica, the Andes as well as a secret polar base near the North Pole. Landig, it is now known, was a Third Reich insider and a member of the Waffen SS. At one time he was responsible for security for the development of German Flying discs.

Landig books each bore the sub-title *Ein Roman voller Wirklichkeiten*, or "a novel filled with realities," as this was an easy avenue in avoiding post-war legal entanglements. Through the descriptions provided by Landig and other records, the Germans not only had a base in Antarctica, but also a large Andean base in Chile. Landig claims that after Operation Highjump, German forces began to abandon Base 211. By the time Admiral Byrd returned in 1958, Base 211 had been abandoned in favor of the Andean base in Chile.

Even more interesting is talk of another secret base located in Greenland. Writers Dr. Milos Jesensky and Robert Lesniakiewicz see the origin of flying saucers over the U.S. during the late 1950s as coming from this forgotten German facility called Beaver Dam in Eastern Greenland.

According to these writers, this base did not surrender with the fall of Germany but continued to function. It was from this base that flying saucers were directed to the U.S. on spy missions, especially toward our nuclear facilities in New Mexico. Additionally, one wonders if this base was the real origin of the ghost rockets seen moving south from Northwestern Europe immediately after the war. The status of this base today is unknown.

We are left with a confusing array of conflicting stories of secret Nazi bases, flying saucers and Admiral Byrd's alleged entry into the hollow Earth. It is safe to conclude that something extraordinary did happen to Byrd in February 1947. The questions that remains are: Did Byrd journey into the hollow Earth through a polar opening? Did he encounter flying discs piloted by inner Earth residents who have been watching the surface world with growing trepidation?

Or, is this story, while partially factual, actually a tale of disinformation to disguise the fact that Admiral Byrd was in Antarctica in 1947 participating in an

Admiral Byrd's Secret Journey Beyond the Poles

operation to seek out and destroy a secret Nazi base? The hollow Earth aspects of this tale may be true. Byrd may have been captured by flying discs, but flown by German pilots. Byrd may have been taken to an underground city, occupied by both surface world Germans and beings from the hollow Earth.

Whatever the case, this tale still leaves us with a lot of unanswered questions. These questions can only be answered by those who are willing to do the serious research, follow the leads and not be afraid of the ridicule or skepticism that is sure to follow.

Admiral Byrd's Secret Journey Beyond the Poles

Did Admiral Byrd encounter Nazi flying discs in Antarctica during Operation Highjump in 1947?

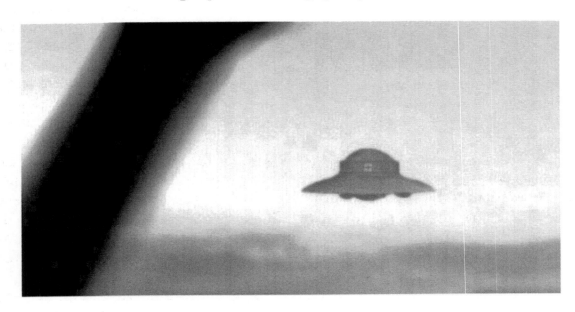

CHAPTER SEVEN
Brooks Agnew – Scientist in Search of Hollow Earth Reality

Brooks A. Agnew, PhD is a commercial scientist and engineer with more than 17 years of field research in Earth Tomography. He also has 15 years of experience creating more than $500 million in process improvements for numerous industries.

His patents have revolutionized photopolymer applications, digital imaging, and high-speed manufacturing processes creating more than five thousand jobs. His technology is used on at least two planets to explore for water and other compounds.

Raised in Pasadena, California Dr. Agnew spent most of his youth hanging around Cal Tech and the folks who worked at the Jet Propulsion Labs. He entered the Air Force in 1973 where he became an electronics engineer. After earning an honorable discharge he attended Brigham Young, Western Kentucky, and Tennessee Technological Universities.

Dr. Agnew has a BS Degree in Chemistry, an MS Degree in Statistics, and a PhD in Physics. He also graduated as class valedictorian in Entrepreneurial Studies and produced a training video on raising money for non-profit ventures.

As a commercial scientist, he has produced thousands of technical papers and numerous patents. He was a featured scientist in the video documentary on *HAARP: Holes in Heaven* directed by Emmy Award Winning Wendy Robbins. He recently co-authored the two national best selling volumes of ***The Ark of Millions of Years***.

Dr. Agnew has recently received substantial attention from the press because of his planned expedition to the Arctic, North Pole Inner Earth Expedition (NPIEE), to hopefully discover the Northern Polar opening to the hollow Earth. The Kentucky based physicist and futurist hopes to board the commercially owned Russian icebreaker Yamal in the port of Murmansk, and to sail into the polar sea just beyond Canada's Arctic islands.

Dr. Agnew is the latest in a long line of people to examine the theory that humans live on the surface of a hollow planet, in which two undiscovered openings, near the North and South poles, connect the outer Earth with an interior realm. However, the original idea to mount a modern-day quest for the Polar opening belongs to the late Steve Currey, a Utah adventure guide who organized rafting trips to the world's wildest white-water rivers. Currey knew how to hype exotic destinations and recruit would-be explorers on trips of a lifetime.

Currey pinpointed the Arctic opening at 84.4 degrees north and 41 degrees east, roughly 250 miles northwest of Ellesmere Island. The inner Earth expedition was scheduled for the summer of 2006, with spaces offered for $20,000.

Admiral Byrd's Secret Journey Beyond the Poles

Dr. Brooks Agnew

Admiral Byrd's Secret Journey Beyond the Poles

When Currey died unexpectedly of brain cancer, Dr. Agnew stepped in to take his place. The trip was postponed and while he insists the journey has a genuine scientific purpose; Dr. Agnew also says the expedition will include several experts in meditation, mythology and UFOs, as well as a team of documentary filmmakers.

However, if nothing is found, Dr. Agnew still promises a grand polar adventure, no matter what the outcome.

"If the polar opening isn't there, the voyage will still make an outstanding documentary," he says. "But if we do find something, this will be the greatest geological discovery in the history of the world."

Dr. Agnew says that much of the Arctic area of planet Earth has never been seen or properly analyzed by humans. Utilizing leading-edge science such as side-scan sonar, dynamo sensing, and gyroscopic global circumference tracking, the team expects to precisely measure the crust and the oceans physical properties to reveal unprecedented features about our planet. Seawater chemistry, marine life cataloging, and even magnetic measurements will be collected during the 13-day expedition to see if there is any hard evidence that might support the hollow Earth hypothesis.

Now, no experiment on this subject would be complete without the other components so vehemently demanded by millions of paranormal prognosticators. There is a multidimensional aspect to this subject matter.

Many believe that there is a void in the interior of the Earth, but that it is fourth, and perhaps even fifth dimensional. These dimensions may require the observer to access higher vibrational levels than the vast sea of seeing-is-believing folks that clog our freeways. There will also be observation effects from the very measurement of these never before seen regions of planet Earth. Something or someone might be disturbed by this process. In other words, if the side-scan sonar sends a pulse across the bow of a 200-foot ship peacefully parked on the floor of the 4200-meter deep ocean, it might relocate itself. Besides being graphed by the sonar software, when that craft moves someone is going to get that movement on film.

QUESTIONS AND ANSWERS WITH BROOK AGNEW

Q: What is your background (education, profession, interests)?

Agnew: I was sort of a permanent student from 1970 until 2000 when I completed my PhD. I started out working as a lab assistant at UCLA Brain Research Institute while my brother was working on his PhD. I have been involved with science or engineering every since. I got my bachelor's degree from Tennessee Technological University in Chemistry. I went to work full time to support my family and worked through the Masters and Doctoral programs using extension and online courses.

Admiral Byrd's Secret Journey Beyond the Poles

My main interest has been manufacturing systems. I have worked for nearly every major auto maker in the U.S., as well as numerous suppliers for the industry. I am a certified quality engineer with a Black Belt in Six-Sigma quality systems.

I co-authored a book on the creation of the Earth in 2005, called *The Ark of Millions of Years*, which rapidly became a national best seller. I began doing radio interviews by demand, and soon was asked to host my own radio program. I founded X-Squared Radio in 2005 and have been growing every since with that wonderful hobby on the BBSRadio Network. We are modeled after Coast-to-Coast AM, but have a distinctly scientific theme with the best guests on Earth.

Q: How did you get interested in the hollow Earth theory?

Agnew: I joined the Inner Earth Expedition in 2005 as a team member to build a gyroscope and help with water sampling and analysis. I was happy to be part of the team. Steven Currey tragically and unexpectedly passed away in the summer of 2006, and I was elected to be the project leader.

Our team looked at the most likely way to fund a $2 million expedition and figured that a documentary film would be the best bet. We did not want to make the film the goal, but then again the world would probably best experience the expedition through film. We calculated that someone with financial backing would see the same incredible value that we did. So far, it has worked out that way.

Q: There is a long history on the idea that the Earth could be hollow, is there any modern science that could suggest the reality of the hollow Earth?

Agnew: The history of the hollow Earth is certainly fascinating and entertaining, but until recently lacked any credible scientific data to back it up. Satellite photos of the Earth have allowed the formation of serious questions and thus hypothesis to be formed about the structure of the planet.

Two things in particular showed up. The first was a photo of the Aurora Borealis over both planetary poles at the same time. This virtually ruled out the idea that this particular phenomenon was caused by the solar wind, a previously assumed source. Second, the USGS seismic data repeatedly, for more than 600,000 reports, produced data inconsistent with the current plate tectonic theory.

Q: Seismic research has shown anomalies that some scientists say could indicate a crust of 800 to 900 miles thick with an open area and then possibly a core of hot iron/nickel – how is this type of research done and who has made these suggestions?

Admiral Byrd's Secret Journey Beyond the Poles

Agnew: When the seismic data is recalculated, using the accelerometer as the starting point and the point of Earthquake as the endpoint, the results are stunning. A clear picture of a planet with a 900 mile thick crust appears in the math models. This, coupled with Washington University study by Dr. Wysessions, produced evidence that another entire ocean may exist underneath the Atlantic Ocean.

There is more. The magnetosphere around Earth is generated by a counter-rotation between two metal bodies. The first is the crust, which is now three times its original post-accretion disc diameter.

The second is the iron core, which was left behind during the overspin condition once the Earth began cooling. The crust is still in a slow expansion, filling with molten magma where the openings to the magma below are formed. By now, as the reader might notice, the crust is stable and cool enough to support liquid water and thus life.

Q: There have been astronomical observations that suggest the Earth is not alone in being hollow. Is there any theory that could explain how the Earth, and other planets, could form with a hollow center?

Agnew: The prevailing theory is that planets form from large accretion discs. These are huge slowly spinning discs of dust and rock. As this mini-galaxy of material becomes attracted to the center, planets begin to form. The Newtonian idea that mass attracts mass, through his concept of gravitation, denotes that in the center, the largest mass collects where the centrifugal forces are weakest. The gravity is believed to be enough to generate enough crushing power to light off the sun.

Now, as we zoom into a single planet, we see a really interesting dynamic process. The dust and rock coagulates into a single body. Obeying the law of conservation of momentum, this little rock spins faster and faster as it gets smaller. We have evidence that one of three things happens.

First, the planet can spin so fast that it explodes. The evidence of this is the plethora of asteroids and free-floating planets we have observed. Second, the planet can spin fast enough to throw off a chunk of itself. This usually exists as a moon. Sometimes that moon can be small enough to stay in orbit, and sometimes it is large enough that it breaks off and forms its own orbit around the central sun. We have evidence of both in our own solar system. Of course, we observe dozens of moons in our own solar system. And, Venus' moon broke off and became Mercury.

The third condition is the gray area in between these two extremes. The crust expands through upheavals, thinning, and cracking. The force releases in the form of heat which melts the inner layers to magma under extreme stress. As the crust cracks open, the magma flows to the outside, cools, and cements the crust back together.

Admiral Byrd's Secret Journey Beyond the Poles

We have clear evidence of this as rock assumes the planet's magnetic alignment at the instant it cools. As the crust expands, the alignment shifts. We have observed igneous rock with a gradient of magnetic fields. This could very well support this theory of crustal expansion.

Why is this important? Because if the crust is expanding, there is another interesting dynamic happening below; let's throw in an Einstein idea here. Suppose you were standing on a bathroom scale in an elevator. That elevator is a shaft that goes to the center of the Earth. When you press the button to go down, you observe your weight on the scale. Sure enough as you approach the center of the Earth, your weight begins to drop. Why? Because all of the mass of the Earth is above you in every direction; like standing on the North Pole, every direction is south.

Now, couple these ideas, and you will see why planets form as spheres and not as solid balls. The crust expands, leaving behind a molten ball of metal, probably iron. The crust is clearly three times its original size, as can be easily seen by fitting all the continental shelves together. The gap left behind is an open void. It filled with air and water. We have historical evidence of cataclysmic periods when the interior of the Earth vented to the exterior of the Earth.

The idea that planets form as hollow spheres is scientifically plausible, but not generally canonized by the high priests of science. Hence, we are mounting an expedition to gather enough observational evidence to either refute or prove the theory.

Q: Why do you think that most geologists ignore such findings preferring to "hang with the pack" refusing even to look at the evidence or speculate beyond the excepted theories of modern geology?

Agnew: It is not so much that they refuse to look at evidence. We have some of the best minds in the world joining our expedition. The problem exists because the approving authorities for PhD's are very conservative, but it goes beyond that. The previous degrees granted are based on things being a certain way. Upsetting that basis for "truth" negates all the previous degrees. In other words, if you got your PhD on the idea that Earth is flat and the sun revolved around the Earth, then sanctioning Galileo's ideas would put your tenure in question. No one wants to be the first to announce that heavier-than-air flight is now possible. Of course, that is irrelevant to those who are looking out the window of their aircraft at the degreed non-fliers below.

Q: What about the theorized holes at the poles? In this age of satellite photography and jetliners supposedly flying over the poles, how could something as obvious as polar openings be kept hidden?

Admiral Byrd's Secret Journey Beyond the Poles

Agnew: Actually, the evidence from both activities is lacking for two reasons. The first is the fact that polar satellites are looking at the Earth from about 260 miles away. They have visible, infrared, magnetic, and x-ray receivers. They are primarily used for weather reporting and thermal reviews of the Earth. The images of the poles don't really exist anymore. The Data Denial Act of 2006 prevents the release of data below 60 degrees latitude to the public. Google Maps animates their data above these areas.

The second reason is that the poles are almost always covered with clouds. This has been the main reason that there is still some credibility to Admiral Byrd's record-breaking polar flight. He flew at an altitude between 1,500 and 2,500 feet. At that altitude, your first mistake is your last.

However, Byrd very likely flew beneath the clouds giving him a clear view of the terrain below. He also would not have had the perspective to know that he was flying into an opening.

The apparent report that Admiral Byrd observed green grass, flowing water, and woolly mammoths where certainly none should have been was what really revived the age-old assertion that the Earth might be hollow. The modern plan to fly across the poles at low altitude is not practical. The cheapest aircraft that could make the 6,000 mile range is a Boeing 727. It would cost about $30,000 for such a trip. The major drawback is that no pilot is going to fly that aircraft for any period of time below 10 thousand feet in altitude. At that altitude, nothing would be visible except clouds.

Q: In your own opinion, do you think that past polar explorers encountered the openings or other anomalies associated with the polar openings?

Agnew: In my opinion, direct observation is excellent evidence. Scientifically speaking, lack of repeatability means the data is not legitimate. Edmund Haley was a strong advocate for the hollow Earth. He had very elaborate theories and great drawings of his ideas. In the 1830's another surge for the theory came out. We think it about a time that someone went to the North Pole and gathered some real hard data and some really good film.

Q: Tell us about the upcoming Arctic trip that you are planning to try and find the Northern opening and other interesting mysteries.

Agnew: The expedition was originally planned by a group lead by Steven Currey. He had a good reputation for exotic and unusual expeditions. Tragically, he died during the preparation of this expedition. I was elected to be the new leader last October. The

Admiral Byrd's Secret Journey Beyond the Poles

original funds collected were refunded by the Currey Estate, and we started over on funding.

The team consists of 100 experts in various fields. We are currently collecting scientists from major universities with expertise in polar research. We have signed experts in diving and arctic filmmaking. Then there is the Indiana Jones aspect of the expedition. In preparing for this trip, some rather powerful and esoteric events happened that convinced us there might be a higher-dimensional aspect to this entire venture. We were convinced, through various means, that we had to address these aspects or the expedition would fail.

Our leadership began training in meditation, light frequency and sound frequency chakra correlations, and even advanced physics for portal cognition. At long last, the project began moving forward extremely rapidly. The supporters for this project have come forth from every side. It seemed as though everyone got the message that we were somehow invited to visit this legendary opening. Perhaps there is an intelligence that knows we are coming and is paving the way and opening doors for us to get there.

There are two entities we have created to accomplish this voyage. The first is a non-profit company called Phoenix Science Foundation:
www.phoenixsciencefoundation.org/APEX.htm
This company is dedicated to bringing forth awareness of new sources of energy technologies and to do planetary explorations. That is where we formed the second company for profit called Advanced Planetary Explorations, LLC. This company owns the film rights, the copyrights and trademarks for the Inner Earth Expedition.

There is a new DVD documentary we produced called *The Inner Earth Expedition Part One.* It is filmed on location at Mount Shasta and in Tibet. There is remarkable footage never before seen in the West that proves beyond any doubt that the idea that the Earth is hollow has roots in ancient history. Couple that with the idea that ancient man has inextricably recorded his involvement with off-world beings, and you have a factor of this story that is simply stunning.

There are three books we have written, and one with which we are participating in a reissue. *The Ark of Millions of Years* has three volumes. They cover the creation and destiny of the Earth, the year 2012 mysteries, and a final book called *Unlocking the Secret.* These are all for sale at all bookstores and Amazon and Barnes & Noble as well as through our website at: **www.arkofmillionsofyears.com**

I am the host of X-Squared Radio, which is the fastest growing talk radio program in North America. The program airs live each Sunday evening from 8:30 to 11:30PM Eastern U.S. time. The archives are available 24/7 at **www.x2-radio.com**

Admiral Byrd's Secret Journey Beyond the Poles

**Satellite photo showing what appears to be
the North Polar opening.**

CHAPTER EIGHT
Is The Hollow Earth in the Fourth Dimension?

In this book we have presented theories and facts on the physical actuality of the inner world; in other words, a place beneath our feet as real and material as you and I. However, there are some who say that the inner Earth is actually outside of the material realm, existing on a higher vibrational level of reality...the fourth dimension.

Consider it this way: the Earth exists as a torus in the third and fourth dimensions. There are two "entrances" into the astral hollow Earth and these are reflected in the physical world as the north and south magnetic poles. Note that the physical North Pole and the magnetic pole are not synonymous in site, but wander in relationship.

The book ***UFO's, Close Encounter of Positive Kind***, which was written with the help of a channeled entity named Jananda, puts it this way. "Question: I don't know if this will fit in with the talk, but lately there has been a lot of news coming out about the inner Earth and about the people there and Admiral Bird in the early part of this century from Walberg, some facility openings at the poles, and that this government helps them. I have been reading a lot of books about that lately. That information seems to be coming out. Is there something I need to know about inner Earth beings?

"Answer: There are beings living on this planet in the inner Earth. They are not all physical. Only a very few of them are physical. They are actually living in the fourth dimension. There are many beings living in the inner Earth. You don't see them. We have another whole world just around us here in another dimension. We have them. So there are a lot of inner Earth people too."

"The planet's inner surface throbs with life and far more life energy than the external one," says RAJ and The Council of The Light, as relayed by Australian-born journalist Peter Farley.

The reason for this is that the inner Sun, which is what holds the planet energetically together, has direct contact with the beings that live on the inner surface of the Earth. Usually the outside of the planet is less protected and has far too much radiation coming from space to keep a healthy level on its surface inhabitants. The inner realm, on the other hand, has no problems with radiation from space sources/stars because the only source of light energy is the planet's heart center: a luminous source of heat/love, light and energy to the inner plane.

The inside of Earth is of a higher vibration and all who live there are pulled into the level of vibration equivalent to fourth and fifth dimensional existence. The shift is somewhat gradual, and those coming from the third dimension would feel lighter and have an easier time breathing.

This is the ascension into fourth dimension that blends the light reflected on physical surfaces into the surfaces themselves, making them more permeable to energy and turning energy reflection into emission of energy. Things become less dense and shadowy. This is not to be confused with the Darkness that controls – that is darkness that limits.

The lessening of shadows on higher realms is due to the change of the behavior of energy and how it is less dense than its materialized third dimensional form. Walking into the inner plane would feel like a soft transition to a dream, but, like a dream, upon leaving the inner world, experiences are forgotten unless the person has enough consciousness development to remember and integrate the memories into the third dimensional brain, or there are measures taken for the remembering to take place. Forgetting can also be helped and some things are forgotten because they were made so. Often it is deemed necessary to not allow memories of the inner world to continue.

The Inner Sun's Light allows for people/animals/different species of beings to receive healing energies directly into their auric fields. Plants grow larger and with juicier fruits. Men and Women live longer, and are better able to develop their spiritual and physical functions.

It is always day and the weather is always warm in the subterranean realm. There is a tale of Viking immigrants that set sail north in search for the land of eternal spring. They did find what they were seeking and it was the inner Earth.

These Viking explorers were right about eternal warm weather, for as you get closer to the North Pole, the climate becomes hotter. There have been expeditions close to the Polar opening that confirm that there are butterflies and less ice the further you travel north. Peoples living in Greenland know of the entrance and natives are aware of travelers from the inner plane that stop by for supplies once in a while.

LANDS BEYOND TIME AND SPACE

Theosophy teaches that a series of seven root-races or humanities will develop during the present fourth round of the Earth's evolution. The first humanity is said to have appeared in the mid-Paleozoic, about 150 million years ago (according to the theosophical timescale), and we are currently in the fifth. Each lives on its own "continent," a word referring not only to the main continental area where the evolution of a root-race takes place but also to all the dry land that exists during the life-period a particular root-race. Just as the root-races overlap, so parts of the continents of one root-race become incorporated into the continental system of the next.

Admiral Byrd's Secret Journey Beyond the Poles

The first continent is known as the Imperishable Sacred Land and is the most mysterious of the seven continents. It is said to be located in the region of the North Pole. This "Sacred Land" is stated never to have shared the fate of the other continents; because it is the only one whose destiny it is to last from the beginning to the end of the Manvantara throughout each Round. It is the cradle of the first man and the dwelling of the last divine mortal, chosen as a Shishta for the future seed of humanity.

Of this mysterious and sacred land very little can be said, except, perhaps, according to a poetical expression in one of the Commentaries, that the 'polestar has its watchful eye upon it, from the dawn to the close of the twilight of a day of the Great Breath. In India this is called The Day of Brahma.

The first continent surrounded and included the North Pole and extended somewhat southwards from the pole in seven different zones, like the leaves of a lotus. These zones included Greenland, Spitzbergen, Sweden, Norway, and Siberia, together with other former land areas in the far north that have since been submerged. The central locality of the first continent was right at the North Pole.

H.P. Blavatsky writes: "If, then, the teaching is understood correctly, the first continent which came into existence capped over the whole North Pole like one unbroken crust, and remains so to this day, beyond that inland sea which seemed like an unreachable mirage to the few arctic travelers who perceived it."

If the Earth is hollow, as Blavatsky implies, then the first continent could refer to two different things: the polar land on the outer surface of the planet and the sacred central land or 'inner circle' in the Earth's interior, which will continue to exist until the Earth reaches the end of its life-period.

Likewise, terms such as "the blessed land of eternal light and summer" and "the land of the eternal sun" could refer either to the polar land at a time when the earth's axis was more or less upright and the polar regions were in sunlight, or to the inner central land if the Earth's interior is self-luminous or contains a central sun.

There is also the consideration that Blavatsky was referring to a land that exists in the astral realms. Many psychics over the centuries state that the higher levels of reality are made up of light and that to live in these realms would be as if living in eternal light. This seems to tie in perfectly to the stories that say the hollow Earth is perpetually lit with the warming rays of a small sun.

Tibetan sacred texts speak of a mystical kingdom called Shambhala, hidden behind snow peaks somewhere north of Tibet, where the most sacred Buddhist teachings – the Kalachakra or Wheel of Time – are preserved. It is prophesied that a future king of Shambhala will come with a great army to free the world from barbarism and tyranny, and will usher in a golden age.

Similarly, the Hindu Puranas say that a future world redeemer, the kalki-avatara, the tenth and final manifestation of Vishnu, will come from Shambhala. Both the Hindu

Admiral Byrd's Secret Journey Beyond the Poles

and Buddhist traditions say it contains a magnificent central palace radiating a powerful, diamond-like light.

The mythical paradise of Shambhala is known under many different names. It has been called the Forbidden Land; the Land of White Waters; the Land of Radiant Spirits; the Land of Living Fire; the Land of the Living Gods and the Land of Wonders.

Hindus have known it as Aryavarsha, the land from which the Vedas come; the Chinese as Hsi Tien, the Western Paradise of Hsi Wang Mu, the Royal Mother of the West; the Russian Old Believers, a nineteenth-century Christian sect, knew it as Belovodye and the Kirghiz people as Janaidar.

However, throughout Asia it is best known by its Sanskrit name, Shambhala, meaning "the place of peace, of tranquillity," or as Chang Shambhala, northern Shambhala, the name Hindus use to distinguish it from an Indian town of the same name. At the end of his life the Chinese Taoist teacher Lao-Tzu, returned to Shambhala, although he called it Tebu Land.

It is regarded by most esoteric traditions as the true center of the planet, as the world's spiritual powerhouse and the heartland of a brotherhood of adepts from every race and country who have been influential in every major religion, every scientific advance and every social movement in history. Buddhist texts say that Shambhala can be reached only by a long and difficult journey across a wilderness of deserts and mountains, and warn that only those who are called and have the necessary spiritual preparation will be able to find it; others will find only blinding storms, empty mountains, or even death.

One text says that the kingdom of Shambhala is round, but it is usually depicted as a lotus blossom with eight-petals, a symbol of the heart chakra. Indeed, an old Tibetan story states that "The kingdom of Shambhala is in your own heart."

As Edwin Bernbaum points out, the guidebooks to Shambhala whose puzzling directions are a mixture of realism and fantasy can be read on one level as "instructions for taking an inner journey from the familiar world of the surface consciousness through the wilds of the subconscious to the hidden sanctuary of the superconscious."

Nicholas Roerich, who was a famous Russian explorer, and mystic, traveled extensively in Tibet and the Himalayas during the 1920s and 30s. Roerich was especially interested in Shambhala, about which he later wrote a book by the same name. Published in 1930, along with *Himalayas: Abode of Light* **and** *Heart of Asia*, Roerich claimed in Shambhala that he possessed a "magical stone from another world" which was known as the Chintamani Stone.

According to David Hatcher Childress, the Chintamani Stone was purported in ancient Asian chronicles to have come from the Sirius star system and is said it been given to Tazlavoo, the one-time Emperor of Atlantis, by an angelic messenger from the

Admiral Byrd's Secret Journey Beyond the Poles

skies. Legend has it that this same stone was sent to King Solomon in Israel, from Tibet via a Vimana airship.

Roerich wrote that Shambhala itself is the Holy Place where the earthly world links with the higher states of consciousness. "Many speculations have been made about the location of the earthly Shambhala. Certain indications put this place in the extreme North, explaining that the rays of the Aurora Borealis are the rays of Shambhala...but this is incorrect. Shambhala is only north in relation to India, being perhaps on the Pamir, in Turkestan, or in the Central Gobi..."

Roerich associates Shambhala with the underground city of Agharta and with the "White Island," and that its "Splendid Valley" is reached via subterranean tunnels and passages from the Himalayas. He further adds that "the underground caverns of Central Asia are inhabited to this day by the people called the Agharti, or Chud, and that when the time of purification comes, say the legends, they will emerge in their glory."

If one can properly describe it as a religion, according to Roerich that of Shambala is of Fire; he relates it to the old cults of Fire and Sun, and the Swastika is its emblem, found carved or painted everywhere. He definitively associates it with the Aryan Race. However, it was not only confined to Buddhist temples. He found it also connected to Bön-Po, a pre-Buddhist Black Faith "which reveres some mysterious gods of the Swastika." He said that they drew the symbol counter-clockwise or left-handed - which, as we've seen, was the version chosen by the Nazis.

Shambhala is the planetary center where the will of Creation is known. It is the most powerful force that pours into our world. Only twice in Earth's history has the Shambhala energy made its presence felt directly. Once during the Lemurian Age, when mankind was suffering a human crisis and secondly in the Days of Atlantis, during a time when there was a great struggle between the Forces of Light and the Forces of darkness.

Through the Shambhala Force, we find that we are not alone to fight the Forces of Darkness. Shambhala's energies are opening our minds and eyes, teaching us that we are not alone in the universe and that there are infinite numbers of other dimensions with civilizations much more advanced than ourselves. The lost Wisdom of the Ages is being returned to us and the old souls are being reincarnated as teachers and guides to help mankind.

World War II was the first evidence of the Shambhala energy, which allowed issues to be brought to light thus creating a change in old traditions. This energy is exceedingly strong and must be spoon fed but so far mankind has done remarkably well under its influence. As time progresses, however, the impact of the Shambhala force will become even more frequent as mankind develops the power to stand and withstand its power.

Admiral Byrd's Secret Journey Beyond the Poles

OTHER REALMS OF THE INNER WORLD

For the past 25 years, Kim Michaels life has been devoted to spiritual growth. During this process, he has worked diligently to establish and sharpen his personal communion with his higher self. Through this communion, he realized that his personal Master, or teacher, is Jesus. Michaels says he was given the gift of direct, inner communion with Jesus, who helped overcome his resistance to serving as his messenger.

In one of his discourses, Jesus explains through Michaels that the material universe exists on four main levels, including the matter realm. As well, there are intelligent beings on all four levels and the four levels are not separated; they simply have different levels of vibration. In other words, they exist in the same "space."

In the matter realm there is no life in the center of the Earth. There are, however, various forms of life, including cities that resemble a paradise, that exist at the other levels of the material universe. There are cities that exist in a space that is congruent with the center of the Earth, just not in the same frequency spectrum as the physical planet.

From time to time, some people have tuned their consciousness to these other realms and have attained a vision of life in the center of the Earth. Because people did not understand the visions, they interpreted that to mean that the Earth was hollow, that there was a sun at the center of the Earth and that there was actual life in the center of the physical planet. In an age with more primitive technology and more limited means of travel, that gave rise to the theory of a hollow Earth. Yet in such matters it can be helpful to simply ask some questions based on common sense. For example, if the Earth was hollow with life living on the inside of the sphere, a sun in the center of the Earth would be so close to the inside of this sphere that it would burn up any form of life.

If the sun was a physical sun, like the sun at the center of the solar system, its heat and nuclear radiation would destroy all life because the Earth is simply too small to give the necessary distance between the sun and the inside of a hollow sphere. One might also reason that with today's technology, including satellites photos and space travel, it would have been impossible to keep the existence of a hollow Earth from becoming common knowledge.

In another frequency spectrum, there is a sun in the center of the Earth, and it is sometimes called the "sun of even pressure." This is a force that balances the material force of gravity. Scientists know that gravity is an accelerating force, so if nothing counterbalanced gravity, the matter of the physical Earth should continue to accelerate in density until it collapsed in upon itself and the Earth became a black hole.

Admiral Byrd's Secret Journey Beyond the Poles

Life does exist in other frequency realms that overlap what in the matter realm is the center of the Earth. Some of those life forms exist in the feeling realm; they have lowered their vibration to a very low level. There is no constructive purpose for connecting with these life forms, although many people insist on doing so despite the danger that is always present.

There are also life forms at the higher levels of the material universe and in the spiritual realm that exist in locations that are congruent with the center of the planet. Such higher beings have indeed created realms that are very similar to the visions of paradise that many people have had through the ages. This is an example of how people can tune their consciousness to a higher frequency spectrum. It can be beneficial for people to connect to such beings, and the process for doing so is the same as for connecting to the Ascended Host. Therefore, there is already such a connection, and we of the Ascended Host are using it to raise the consciousness of the planet as much as possible.

There are many areas on this planet, especially in large cities, where a large number of people have developed such imbalances in their emotional bodies that the entire area vibrates at the level of the feeling realm. The feeling realm currently has the lowest vibrations of any of the realms. Some areas of the feeling realm are literally what people have seen as Hell. Therefore, there are areas on this planet that vibrate at the level of the feeling realm. These areas are literally Hell on Earth.

Likewise, there are areas that resonate with the thought realm. An example are institutions of learning in which people have glorified the human intellect, yet have denied the higher reasoning of the Christ mind. Finally there are areas, such as areas devoted to spiritual activities that are attuned to the etheric realm or even the spiritual realm. Such areas are Heaven on Earth.

So you see, once again, that human beings have the ability to create their own reality. You create that reality through the power of the mind, yet to understand how, you need to recognize that your mind has several levels. Your lower mind is very much like a radio receiver that simply amplifies radio frequencies and makes them detectable to the senses. What you create through the lower mind is determined by what streams into that mind from the higher levels of the mind.

The question now is to which station the radio of your mind is tuned? Is it tuned to your Christ self, or is it tuned to beings in the lower realms? You must choose this day who you will serve. You must choose in which mansion in my Father's house you want to live, and you decide that by focusing your attention on a certain level. If you have an imbalance in your lower bodies, you will focus on the material, the feeling or the thought realm. If your identity body is unbalanced, you will focus on the identity realm without reaching higher. Yet if all of your four lower bodies are balanced, you can reach beyond the identity realm and commune with the Ascended Host.

Admiral Byrd's Secret Journey Beyond the Poles

You can then become the open door for bringing the vibrations and the truth of Heaven to Earth. You can become the open door for the Living Word to stream into this world.

T. LOBSANG RAMPA'S JOURNEY TO THE INNER EARTH

For several decades, books by the Tibetan mystic T. Lobsang Rampa have brought spiritual enlightenment to millions worldwide who may have never had the chance to learn of Buddhism and the unique magical qualities of the mysterious land of Tibet. In his book *My Visit to Agharta* (2003, Inner Light Publications), Rampa travels to the hollow Earth through a strange vortex in time and space. When he emerges from the other side, he is amazed to find himself in a world that exists in a higher vibrational realm of reality.

From our perspective it appeared as if we were standing in the middle of a great bowl of fantastic size. Instead of a horizon, the land curved upwards and away from us in all directions to finally become lost in the turquoise blue sky above. In the center of the sky there hung a sun of magnificent beauty. Somewhat smaller and dimmer than the sun of our solar system, but still casting a splendid soft, golden brightness that illuminated the entire landscape with its holy luminance.

The land was rich in beauty and life. In an almost tropical environment, flowers of all types grew in profusion throughout. Their perfume wafted on the breeze bringing an almost childlike delight to my sense of smell as I remembered sweet days of youth. Streams of crystal clear water flowed and bubbled through the forests and grasslands. The air was alive with the sounds of birds and insects whose songs rose and fell with the universal rhythm of all life. In the distance I could see great and beautiful cities with buildings that seemed to defy the law of gravity. The structures, which gave the appearance of being made from beautiful clear crystal and gemstones, glowed with the incredibly radiant light of cosmic grandeur.

Until he spoke up, I had almost forgotten the Master who stood beside me equally in awe of the sight before us.

"Behold," he said magnificently, "sacred Agharta."

Many believe that Agharta is a city in the center of the Earth. However, Agharta is actually the name of the entire land and not one single city. Here resides Earth's cosmic power. All powers of matter, energy and time-space dimensions achieved by living creatures, originate from this cosmic source. In this land live a number of races with disparate cultures

Admiral Byrd's Secret Journey Beyond the Poles

and traditions. They live in a much more evolved and advanced dimension compared with human life on the surface, in perfect symbiosis with the planet and its living reality.

Other races other than those from Earth also occupy the interdimensional land of Agharta. Here there are large colonies of extraterrestrial peoples originating from many diverse places in our universe. These groups also interrelate at different dimensional levels.

The capital of Agharta is the etheric city of Shamballa. This city is the highest expression of this internal civilization and vibrates at astral frequencies. There, the creative idea and the astral program for the Earths evolution are conceived and instituted. In Shamballa dwell extraordinary beings that vibrate at the highest frequencies of the universe. They are free beings, owners of life. They build destiny. They live together in large clans, guided by the Elders. The eldest clan is the keeper of the Word. The elder of this clan is the Directing Mind of all life inside and outside the planet.

They exist on higher frequencies, totally free of the temporal system. Going through time planes, they are subjected to their effects only so long as they are immersed in them. But their entity remains unchanged in its immortal nature. They are the Alpha and Omega of all life in the universe.

They wear rich, light clothing of encompassed beauty and art, laced with gold and multicolored arabesques. They are taller than the average human with strong and extremely vital features that could be likened to those of the Polynesian people.

Unfortunately, we were not pure enough to visit Shamballa. Even though we were able to transcend our surface world vibrational state and enter Agharta, we were still far removed from those pure souls who dwelt in Shamballa. But our reason for being here was not for sightseeing. We had another purpose, a purpose that was soon to be revealed to all.

We joined the multitude of enlightened beings who had collected on the great plain at the foot of the dimensional doorway. Above us in the sky soared great spherical vessels that dipped and dodged in the breeze like the kites of Lhasa.

"Look in the sky," the Master pointed out. "Those are soul crafts made up of pure thought and capable of traveling anywhere in this universe."

The air was vibrant with excitement as the sound of billions of voices drifted over the landscape. All who were here knew that this was a momentous occasion in the history of the present universe and felt honored and humble to be a part of it.

Admiral Byrd's Secret Journey Beyond the Poles

"Incredible, there are so many," I said out loud. "The world can scarcely hold us all."

The Master laughed a rich, deep laugh of utter joy and delight, something that I had never heard him do in all the years that I knew him on the surface world.

"Look around us Lobsang," the Master said as he spread out his arms. "Beings from all worlds and all times have come together at this one point in infinite time and space. It is a miracle that I had scarcely dreamt possible, yet here we all are. But you shouldn't worry about Agharta overflowing with enlightened beings, because this place sits in the center of both the material and astral planes of existence. Not only is it located in the center of our planet, it is also located in the centers of millions of other planets. Agharta is in the heart of all conscious beings throughout the universe."

For those who have trouble believing that the hollow Earth is real, Rampa, and others who are more spiritually enlightened have no problems understanding that the underground realms exist not only in the third dimensional physical world, but also in other dimensional realities. Because it exists outside time and space as we know it, the inner world can be accessed from different points in the universe.

These "warp" points, due to gravity and the effects of mass on time/space, commonly exist underneath the surface of planets with the north and south regions being particularly prone to shifts in the walls that normally separate the different vibrational worlds. This is one reason why the myths and legends of mankind describing fantastic underground worlds are so prevalent and universal.

CHAPTER NINE
Worlds Within Worlds
By Dr. Wendy Lockwood, PH.D.

Know this: All spherical natural celestial bodies are hollow. Someday that will be one of man's greatest rediscoveries, besides who and where God is. The centuries-old theories expounded by today's scientists as Truth, must be reformed into reality if humankind is to continue to progress.

Our current scholars, through peer pressure and the desire to be socially accepted as, (just another bee in the hive), has retarded the pioneer spirit to rediscover amazing new frontiers. Also, so many factions of society have placed stock in, and dependency upon the standard, and even obsolete commodities such as fossil fuels, to support their own prosperity, that, in many cases general progress is now delayed or even halted. Fear and power-tactics suppresses and oppresses the inspired genius who steps forth with a pure heart, offering a better way, and thus challenging the old establishment. It is disgraceful that such powers have been allowed to thrive at the expense of human progress, just to satisfy greed and glut. Humanity suffers when it is not permitted to advance at any level. That is contrary to life's purpose and Cosmic Law.

All we have to do is consider the past fifty years compared to the previous fifty. The first half of the twentieth century contributed a non-stop flow of inventions and civilized advancement. Mankind excelled in all -directions. Then, along came computers. From what we have been told, the computer is the result of back engineering from the so-called "flying saucer physics," not necessarily an original or inspired concept. Computers should enhance our inner & outer evolution; not to dominate us.

Those vessels which were either captured or retrieved from UFO crash sights, such as the Roswell, New Mexico incident, have allegedly been sources from which many of our technological "progresses" were derived, In other words, those sources may not have been from the creative genius-inventory at least since the pre-deluvian age some hundred thousand years ago. There is nothing new under the sun.

For over a hundred years, the traditionally dyed-in-wool, programmed scientists and professors have apathetically presented theory as fact. What has happened to the thrill of discovery and the acceptance of major new concepts? We can credit those who are at the root of society. Those roots are withering away. However, there is some hope, and that is the renewal of ethics and honesty in the media. As we know, the media can be used to degenerate or advance mankind. It is critical that positive reality and truth is presented through those channels, because the erroneous nature of the human mind

Admiral Byrd's Secret Journey Beyond the Poles

tends to accept all as truth, thus the corruption is easily planted in the mind, as fact. That is because very few people have enough intuition or know-how to use it, or to sort-out reality. They don't even know what intuition is.

To the majority of mankind, the media is the primary mundane source of factual information, including the Internet, (more so than our educational institutions). Of course unfortunately, most of the movies, television, computer sources and even the words written into music, are subject to leading the naive astray. Most of humankind does not recognize truth from deceit. Most want to be absorbed into illusion because it feels good and they are lazy.

Therefore, when a new concept is presented, which is very unfamiliar, and it does not fit into the familiar data banks, we will tune it out, deny it, or call it "evil." Certain divisions of civilization are constantly digging in their heels and blinding themselves to any new frontiers. They will do all they can to place obstacles and smoke screens before advancement and gain based upon preservation of their often-opulent life styles. The new scientists of this age will reveal those ancient truths, long hidden from mankind. "Truth is stranger than theory" and certainly far more wondrous. That process is beginning even now, and as the young future scientists mature, the old obsolete scholars will let go, some even incarnating as the New Eden Scientists.

Those souls will help restore the truths of our worlds and the mystery of man. Theory will step aside for truth, and the truth will free us from ignorance, stagnation and degeneracy. It will restore the ethics empowering mankind with the innocence and our original Adamic God-status.

At last we shall know the true structure of our planet and other worlds, not just from hearsay, but also from discovery and experience. We will know that the old myth of planets having solid-molten cores is timeworn quackery. It is far more difficult to prove a molten core exists than the planet is hollow. In fact, that has already been proven by certain portions of the government, but has not been publicly released.

Certainly NASA knows there are polar entrances and I believe the HAARP project in Alaska may be directed at seeking out ways to penetrate that great inner world. The original reason given by HAARP was to search out subterranean polar spaces. The Hubble telescope and polar satellite have produced amazing glimpses beyond the falsely hung veils placed before the eyes of our so-called "civilization."

The ancients had a far greater grasp on the truth than we have in our culture. If we could compare our present status to that of Atlantis, at its height, we would be humbled and awakened to a new perspective, (that we have a long way to go).

Admiral Byrd's Secret Journey Beyond the Poles

The space within Eden is about 6,400 miles in diameter. The inner sun is about 600 miles across. Eden is an exquisite magic land, full of beauty and harmony. The atmosphere of pale sparkling gold is always fragrant. The other holy secret cities are created on the same principles.

Illustration by Dr. Wendy Lockwood

Admiral Byrd's Secret Journey Beyond the Poles

The Great Ones perceive us as barbaric and savage. Mankind has far to go and a short while to achieve a higher state of consciousness before the great global purging. This planet has recovered from vast changes, from continental drifts, quakes, polar shifts, rising and sinking of lands, moon falls, the icefall from the frozen mists around the world, nuclear wars from the ancient past as well as now, invasions of terrestrials and extraterrestrials, even far more over the past six ages.

It has been bombarded with unspeakable horrors. Each age concluded with a fall of civilizations caused by a wave of souls, mostly from Mars. Those souls are always of a lower state of consciousness. While the evolved souls move on up to Venus, Mercury, and the Sun, the Martians inherit the old culture and always it collapses into corruption, war and ultimately, destruction because those souls are so negative, ignorant and competitive.

That is happening presently upon our earth, but this time there will be a different process because this is our last and Seventh Age. After the purging, all rebellious, negative souls will be removed from this and every world in the cosmos.

By then, the remaining soul-bearing beings will be weary of error and never ending useless wars. When we are so beat-down into the dust by our own self-righteous arrogance, greed, passions and competition, only then will we reach out and confess that we cannot learn by our own man-made laws, doctrines and principles. Then and only then will the soul's impulses be heard rather than the growl of the beast. Only then will the soul-bearing beings humbly and respectfully ask for truth and guidance, and they shall mercifully receive it.

We are arriving at the time of disclosure. Some of us already know the truths and we will be those who shall reveal it to others, showing them how to prove it. Even the Bible states in first Thessalonians, 5:21, "Prove All Things." That clearly states, we must have faith, but faith in that which we have proven not someone's theory or biased interpretations or interpolation.

There are many in this world who knows by experience, (by proof), that this planet and all worlds are hollow spheres. Knowledge is power when it is correctly directed to benefit humankind. Mankind's greatest enemy is stupidity and ignorance. A person can be a life long scholar with many degrees and if that person fills their skull cavity with useless theories, trivia and false or negative data, they may as well be an illiterate or brainless person. When we are rigid to new discoveries and concepts, we halt our spiritual growth and begin to age rapidly, we degenerate.

Now, there is a universe of evidence that planetary bodies are hollow, by the law of physics. That is not equaled by the opposite theory of molten planetary cores.

For ages, varied civilizations have taught that the earth is a hollow sphere or at least full of "holes." Those beliefs have been recorded throughout the archives of time around the world, translated into symbolical stories, mythologies, fairy tales, and even sacred scriptures.

In the Christian Bible, The King James version, we are told in Job, 26:7, "He stretched out the North over the empty place and hangeth the earth upon nothing." Again, in Isaiah, 24:1, it states, "Behold, the Lord maketh the earth empty", and in Zechariah, 6:7, it states, "An the bay (horse) went forth and sought to walk to and fro through the earth; and he said, "get you hence, walk to and fro through the earth. So they walked to and fro through the earth."

THERE ARE OPENINGS AT THE POLES

It is a fact that the Aurora Borealis is the light emitted from the Inner Eden and northern Shamballa. Part of the light is reflected from the rainbow beams of the city and the central Sun. As the ancient wisdom teachings tell us, that city is called Northern Shamballa or Kadoth. There are also southern lights, but the northern are brighter due to the crystal city and positive polarity.

I have a collection of photos made from the polar satellite, the Venus probe by the Soviet Union and the Hubble telescope. These are photos revealing the polar openings on each planet. When we understand what we are looking at, then they become very evident.

I also have photos from the space shuttle over the Northern polar opening. Often there are clouds in those great apertures; warm cloud formations from the tepid inner terrarium-like atmosphere, which are drawn to the cold polar air. The contrast and global rotation often causes them the spin in a pinwheel formation in their warm and cold wind-dance with each other. Often there is a defined margin around the vast cloud lid. If our governments deny the polar portals, then they are further deceiving mankind.

The Martian polar ice caps, I believe, have or will be discovered as auras glowing through those entrances, illuminating the ice caps. It appears that the Mars ice caps are considerably smaller than earth's. Proportionately, the depth of those ice caps would have to be about fifty miles thick (as) portrayed in the photos). There appears to be vast bubbles over the openings, which is the light distribution from the inner sun. All cosmic and natural globes are hollow.

When a planet is first conceived, there are negative-positive cross beams and where they meet at a junction point is the focus of creation that attracts cosmic dust which coagulates into solid form. At first it is a glowing point of life-giving light. As it expands, the whirling motion separates the locked core from the heavier matter creating a solid outer shell. The energies from the beams form the openings. The denser matter is formed outward and the lighter remains centered.

Admiral Byrd's Secret Journey Beyond the Poles

After the ages pass, the planetary body becomes habitable, at least within. There are so many variations of life, which supports a universal soul unit, that any possible form of life could thrive on a planet, depending upon the molecular basis of the being. They may not even appear as a life-form according to our standards.

On Mercury there is a soul-bearing being, which resembles a great crystal. Let me include, Mercury is not hot, it is ice-clad. One great fallacy of our scientists is that space conducts heat from the Sun. For one thing, the Sun is not hot. The flames we see are the flames of interdimensional Divine Fire. The Sun is theoretically activated by cold fusion.

We have seen comets approach the Sun at a very close distance; yet maintain their icy cores. There have been space probes sent to orbit the Sun, which did not incinerate. If the Sun was hot, space would be hot, but Mercury is not hot and space itself is zero degrees.

It matters not whether a planet is near or far from the Sun, what the temperature is. The planetary temperatures are determined by the chemical contents of the atmosphere and the Sun's ionic radiation interacting with the atmosphere. The Sun casts off negative ions, which are life giving and beneficial. The positive, deadly ions cast off the Sun are actually bounced off the Sun's from channels in space and cast into the solar systems to be absorbed upon the planets. There is only one place in space which does not absorb those deadly rays, and that is the Pleiades and the Photon Belt around and in its vicinity because that space partakes of fourth dimensional qualities.

Present day scientists do not understand space. The Great Masters tell us that space is 9-dimensional and actually solid, except when an object passes through it, certain corridors are followed. The future compression of space and all within will be drastically different from today's theory, when this planet returns to peace and Paradise. Presently man is too barbaric to receive such detailed information about the density of space. When a block of pure silver is reduced to zero degrees, it becomes transparent. (Silver is a protective metal when worn).

Planets are not cast-offs of suns. Each one is a separate creation upon a crossbeam. Even man-made orbiting bodies in which beings reside must be hollow. The moon is hollow, as we know, cast forth from the great Pacific Basin near the Caroline Islands, by the Masters of the White Lodge to shield us from Erlik the dark star also placed in orbit by the Serpent Race or Zetas. The moon is a spaceship and is steered to block the dark star. The moon is a White Lodge outpost a sentinel to protect our planet. Each planet moves within its own ninth dimensional corridor. One way a planet can be displaced is if it were blasted into smithereens and forced beyond the ninth dimensional barriers by sheer molecular frequency and then cast back into matter because of its fundamental negative or three dimensional qualities.

The asteroid belt from the planet Eros was formed in that manner. Eros was a former abode of the Zetas or Serpent Race. The White Lodge obliterated Eros because

Admiral Byrd's Secret Journey Beyond the Poles

the Dracos-Zetas- Serpent Race were consuming all human flesh on that planet and had designs to invade Earth with the same goals. The Serpent Race is the epitome of evil, breaking all Cosmic Laws. They have a diabolical immortality limited to the material planes, by some, being called "perfectly evil," or a negative-perfect.

Eros is where the Chinese race originated. They were the victims of the Serpent Race. As previously described, the survivors fled to our moon where they took refuge for a while and then proceeded on to China (in their cigar space ships), establishing that territory as their land. The legends of the flying dragon is based upon the spaceships), that carried them safely to earth. It is said, that some cigar ships are hidden away in a cave somewhere in China. The Serpent Race had already invaded Earth, but more waves of them followed. Some set up bases on Mars and others actually survive on certain larger asteroids.

The Polar entrance to Saturn is very clear and on Venus it is also sharply defined. The Russian probe to Venus photographed a great opening. Most of Venus's life is within the hollow center. There is some external life which cannot be measured by Earth's standards of life. The inner world of Venus is like a continual rain forest. There are no seasons, but humanoid life does thrive in that world.

Within each central planetary hollow is where the White Lodge establishes headquarters on each mortally inhabited world. The inner spaces are pure because the deadly ions are cast-off through the entrances leaving only the life-giving energy there. Those who live within therefore are usually immortal. The deadly ions bouncing off our Suns are the cause of the fall, evil, insanity, disease, crime, aging and death. It affects the mind first and blocks soul expression. Keeping a negative ion generator near us actually helps promote longevity and harmony by neutralizing the positive deadly ions.

The word, "Holy" is derived from "hollow" because the hollow world is sacred within. Our present outer Holy land is the namesake of ancient America, which was called the "Holy Land" during the reign of Atlantis, which lasted a couple hundred thousand years. America, at that time was called Galilee and Lake Superior was the Sea of Galilee.

All beneath America were vast cavern networks carved out or enhanced by the Atlanteans in preparation for an "Armageddon" or vast anticipated earth changes. Those caves were stocked with food, machines, cultural centers, parks, palaces, transworld highways and every need for survival from a poisoned or devastated world.

The Great Masters had foresight of the Great Flood and Polar Shifts, however, when those upheavals began, most White Lodge and enlightened Masters chose to evacuate earth for more pure worlds. Some remained behind. They numbered 144. They took refuge in the seven secret cities, surrounded by 4th-dimensional space warps, including the twelve smaller cities.

Admiral Byrd's Secret Journey Beyond the Poles

That vast cavern network beneath America was then occupied by the lower evolved races that fled the earth changes. They were essentially ignorant and very negative. They were called the DERO, from which the word "devil" was derived. The Dero learned to use and abuse the technology down there, such as healing "mech," teleportation devices and telogs, to spy on the surface. Those mech can penetrate through 50 miles of solid granite.

Many so-called ghosts and UFOs are holograms projected by the Dero to the surface. They are also responsible for causing pain and suffering to those of us who live on the surface. By using their machines, the Dero cause terrible accidents for their amusement.

The late Richard S. Shaver was my mentor for pre-Deluvian art and historical, sub-surface training. He was kidnapped and taken into the Dero caves where they enslaved him as a mechanic to repair the ancient mech.

He was down there in that hell for years and was exposed to a surreal Hades. He told of entrances to those caves beneath all major cities in America and networked-out beneath all primary cities of the world including close connections to the Vatican's sub-basement elevators and tunnels.

The Holy Land in the near East is named after the holy land of America, or the original Galilee. Then American's holy land title was borrowed from the holey-holy earth within. The present near eastern Holy Land earned its name because it is vastly honeycombed, (down to the Dero-caves) with layer upon layer of cities and caverns. It is not truly a sacred land. It was occupied by Moses and Jesus, as well as other holy souls because it was so very negative under the Dero-watch and control.

The Deros can control the mind and place thoughts in an unshielded person. They can inject voices as heard by schizophrenics and criminals whom they follow all through their lives via the Telogs or spy mech. The Dero have very little to do but make devilish trouble for surface man. Because they send the ray-mech up to the surface to reflect the sun's light into the caves, the deadly ions are multiplied and that results in monsters, mutated by radiation, mad as maniacs who get their life long kicks out of confusing man's mind and creating havoc. These too shall be destroyed in the earth changes.

So, as you can see, the earth must first be purged and all evil souls must be exiled. Combined with the release of the demons from the seventh dimension, the serpent race and the influence of the Anti Christ, is it any wonder mankind is controlled as puppets in the deadly dance of evil?

When man fell, he forgot his God-self and lost all cosmic wisdom, therefore he is a perfect target for deceit. That is why the Great Masters of the White Lodge are here; to send out regular emissaries, gurus or Messiahs to reeducate the misled and confused minds. To set straight all misunderstanding so that through man's inherent (mighty God-Powers) we can be reactivated and overcome the darkness that invaded our

Admiral Byrd's Secret Journey Beyond the Poles

consciousness ten million years ago. It's been a long time since we've been home, but if you are reading this dear one, you're on your way back.

Admiral Byrd called the inner earth of Northern Shamballa or Kadoth, "the land of everlasting mystery." We are told that the entrances or polar openings are about 14,000 miles in diameter. The Earth's crust is about 800 miles thick and center of gravity rests at about 400 miles below. There is more occupied land on the inner earth than the outer, and more people live within the Dero caverns than on the surface. Dr. Doreal taught about the Deros.

The original NASA photos of the Earth that were taken from the Moon, clearly reveals the polar entrances. By the second printing they were doctored to conceal them. I believe that public exposure to any further Moon ventures are now concealed, redirecting attention to dramatic Earth events. Too much was revealed about the Earth's true form and other space anomalies.

The dark forces are blocking mankind's knowledge of the inner Eden because it is a very severe threat to them and their agenda to man. The Masters want man to know about Eden, which will stir his interest in the roots of Truth and accelerate our wisdom, knowledge and Enlightenment.

The space within Eden is about 6,400 miles in diameter. The inner sun is about 600 miles across. Eden is an exquisite magic land, full of beauty and harmony. The atmosphere of pale sparkling gold is always fragrant. The other holy secret cities are created on the same principles.

When I visited Eden through bi-location I was blissfully consumed at the wonders. There are mountains, rivers, and lakes. Most of the mountains are clad in evergreens. The grass is always green and wild flowers bloom everywhere. Fruit trees are in all stages of production because there are no seasons. Everything grows gigantic, even the animals and holy beings who dwell there. I walked through a meadow with flowers that towered over my head; petals that were opalescent transparent and pure perfume to breath. All is in Divine Harmony in Eden. The lion lies down with the lamb and no beast is at odds with the others.

As I gazed upward, I beheld the central sun shrouded in mists, glowing through and beyond the inner mantle of the Eden rose up and the mountains and lakes seemed to fade into the sky. The Aurora Borealis is the light from the inner sun and Shamballa glowing above the top of the world.

Someday we will all enter that magic world in our process of enlightenment. The gates will be open, free for us to pass through. But first we must pass through the purging procedure to remove all corrupt influences and entities from this beautiful planet.

You can play a part in that by following the path I've laid before you. Nobody ever truly dies...we just change garments and from now on, most incarnating souls will remember their past lives, thus giving them a quantum leap forward in their Enlightenment. By so doing, we will be permitted to enter the holy cities and Eden to study at the feet of the greatest Masters.

Know this, dear reader, at this time in history; nobody can enter Eden or the holy cities, except by invitation. There are tremendous space warps around all the holy places of the Great White Lodge and any forced attempt to enter will instantly send the trespasser to another planet by teleportation. We qualify by the degree of devotion and sincerity of our inner growth. We have a free will to break the circle and rise into a spiral, freeing ourselves once and for all, of the fallen, miserable, suffering ignorant state of consciousness. The majority of the fallen have, already overcome and so can you. The Kingdom of Heaven is WITHIN YOU and the INNER EARTH.

Admiral Byrd's Secret Journey Beyond the Poles

**UFOs have been seen all over the world flying in and out
Of underground tunnels.**

Illustration by Carol Ann Rodriguez

CHAPTER TEN
The Rainbow City – UFOs From the Inner World

Mankind's earliest myths and legends speak of incredible cities that are home to the gods and other enlightened beings. These mystical cities are said to be found all across the planet, usually beyond the highest mountains, over the deepest oceans, through the most impenetrable jungles, or even in the subterranean world.

A modern version of the "lost cities of the gods" connects the UFO phenomena along with the hollow Earth in an interesting revision of the ancient legends of a superior race that remains hidden by choice from the rest of the world.

Author Brinsley Le Poer Trench, who wrote *Lost Atlantis Inside the Hollow Earth* (Reprinted 2006, Inner Light Publications) presents the idea that Man who according to the Biblical book of Genesis came from within the ground and not just as dust as is taught by mainstream religions. In earlier books Le Poer Trench postulated that a number of the Elchim (gods) had indulged in a breeding experiment. This went wrong and they were expelled, along with the race of Adam. These were the fallen angels, giants, Anunnaki - the Nephilim of the Bible.

William F. Warren, in a scholarly work *Paradise Found, or The Cradle of the Human Race at the North Pole*, quotes from a translation by A-M- Sayce taken from a book called *Records of the Past*: "We are told of a dwelling which the gods created for the first human beings on Earth – a special dwelling in which they became great and increased in numbers and the secret location of which is described in words exactly corresponding to those of Iranian, Indian, Chinese, Eddaic and Aztecan literature; namely, in the center of the Earth."

Bal Gangadhar Tilak (1856-1920), a renowned pioneer protagonist of Indian Independence at the turn of the 20th century, was also a scholar in astronomy and Vedic antiquities, who among other feats, was able to place the oldest Indian Vedic civilization at around 4500 BCE. Tilak was jailed by the British for his anti-British writings for several years, and this time he put to good use in studying the Veda scripts, in relation to known astronomical and geological events.

Tilak published his findings in a book called *The Arctic Home of The Vedas* in 1903. In this he stated that, according to his readings of the Vedas, the original Arctic home of humanity was destroyed around 10,000 - 8,000 BCE by the last Ice Age, and that from 8,000 - 3000 BCE, was the "Age of Wandering," before they Vedic people finally settled in India between 5,000 - 3000 BCE. By then, he went on to add, they had already begun to forget their Arctic origins and traditions.

Admiral Byrd's Secret Journey Beyond the Poles

Ancient Indian texts seem clearly indicate that the Arctic region was the "realm of the ancient gods" since they specifically mention that it is where the sun rises and sets only once a year – which demonstrates that the writers had a clear knowledge of the astronomical and seasonal situation at the North Pole. The question here is how did the ancient Indians know this?

The obvious answer is because it was recorded in the Vedic Hymns, which speak of "The Dawn of Many Days" and "The Thirty Dawn Sisters Circling Like A Wheel." When applied to the North Pole, these terms make sense since the sun takes exactly a month to actually appear above the horizon after the four-month night.

These ancient forebears of the Indian people, the Aryans, obviously knew from first-hand experience that the sun takes a further month each year, to set. So there's a polar twilight of one month, followed by a night of four months then a dawn of one month, followed by a day of four months. Even though the details were written thousands of years ago, the Vedas are absolutely correct.

The oldest Vedic year had only two divisions, which were called devas and pitras; names which correlated with the "Day of The Gods" and the "Night of The Gods." This, curiously enough, is very reminiscent of another dramatic piece of Germanic Aryan mythology, Gottdammerung, the "Twilight of The Gods" which is a strangely apt connection with the Vedic-Aryan Polar Year.

If the ancient Aryans did originate from a great city located in the hollow Earth, how did they arrive on the surface world to begin with? Obviously they couldn't have walked the entire distance, but Vedic traditions offer a possibility that may also serve as a clue to the modern question of the origin of UFOs.

FLYING MACHINES FROM THE INNER WORLD

In the Vedic literature of India, there are many descriptions of flying machines that are generally called vimanas. Usually they are described as manmade craft that resemble airplanes and fly with the aid of birdlike wings and unusually shaped structures that fly in a mysterious manner and are generally not made by human beings. The word vimana is purportedly derived from vamana: "He who is able at three strides to take measure of the entire Earth and heavens."

India's national epic, *The Mahabharata*, is a poem of vast length and complexity. According to Dr. Vyacheslav Zaitsev: "The holy Indian Sages, the Ramayana for one, tell of two storied celestial chariots with many windows that roar off into the sky until they appear like comets. *The Mahabharata* and various Sanskrit books describe at length these chariots, saying that they are "powered by winged lighting...it was a ship that soared into the air, flying to both the solar and stellar regions."

Admiral Byrd's Secret Journey Beyond the Poles

Col. Henry S Olcott, who was a cofounder of the Theosophical Society, said in 1881 during a lecture in Allahabad: "The ancient Hindus could navigate the air, and not only navigate it, but fight battles in it like so many war-eagles combating for the domination of the clouds. To be so perfect in aeronautics, they must have known all the arts and sciences related to the science, including the strata and currents of the atmosphere, the relative temperature, humidity, density and specific gravity of the various gases..."

The *Arthasastra of Kautilya* (c. 3rd century BCE) mentions amongst various tradesmen and technocrats the Saubhikas as "pilots conducting vehicles in the sky." Saubha was the name of the aerial flying city of King Harishchandra and the form Saubika means "one who flies or knows the art of flying an aerial city."

Kautilya uses another significant word "Akasa Yodhinah," which has been translated as "persons who are trained to fight from the sky." The existence of aerial chariots, in whatever form it might be, was so well-known that it found a place among the royal edicts of the Emperor Asoka which were executed during his reign from 256 - 237 BCE.

The *Vaimanika Shastra* refers to about 97 works and authorities of ancient times of which at least twenty works deal with the mechanism of aerial flying machines, but none of these works is now traceable. The *Yuktikalpataru of Bhoja* includes a reference to aerial cars in verses 48-50 and a manuscript of the work belonging to the Calcutta Sanskrit College dated at 1870 CE

From these ancient texts it is clear that there were sophisticated vimanas, or aircraft in ancient India and they followed the route over the western sea i.e. Arabian Sea - Africa - Atlantic ocean - Latin America/Mexico. Other airships might have also followed this route, but most of the cargo ships had to follow the longer route over the Pacific Ocean via Indonesia - Polynesia - Latin America/Mexico because of the favorable trade winds and the equatorial currents that made navigation easier.

Prof. D. K. Kanjilal analyses the legend of the *Matsya Purana* (chapters 129) in his **Vimana in Ancient India** in the following words: "Behind the veil of legend and scientific truth comes out that three flying-cities were made for and were used by the demons. Of these three, one was in a stationary orbit in the sky, another moving in the sky and one was permanently stationed in the ground. These were docked like modern spaceships in the sky at particular time and at fixed latitude/longitudes. Siva's arrow obviously referred to a blazing missile fired from a flying satellite specially built for the purpose and the brunt spaceship fell in the Indian Ocean. Vestiges of onetime prosperous civilization destroyed in battles only flicker through these legends."

Many modern researchers attribute the vimanas and the technology that accompanied them as proof that the ancient world was being visited by extraterrestrial beings. However, upon closer examination of The Puranas and other ancient Vedic traditions, it is clear that the vimanas were brought to the surface world when the Aryans migrated from their inner world home before the last ice age.

The French esoteric writer, Saint-Yves d'Alveydre, in 1886 revealed in his book, **Mission of India**, that the ancient Aryans came from Agartha, which is a hidden land beneath the surface of the Earth. This inner world was ruled over by a black sovereign Pontiff called the Brahmatma. This realm saw a migration to the surface world around 3,200 BC, at the beginning of the Kali Yuga (or Golden Age) and that Agartha has known technology such as artificial lighting, mechanized transport, and even air-travel, far in advance of our own modern technology. The surface world would often trade with Agharta using vimanas to fly in and out of secret tunnels that connected the hollow Earth with the surface.

Even today, Agartha sends emissaries to the upper world, about which it keeps astonishingly well informed. Agartha also has huge libraries which enshrine the whole wisdom of the ages, engraved in stone. Many great secrets lie there, regarding many esoteric and spiritual subjects, including amazing skills and abilities long-forgotten by those who dwell on the surface.

SUBTERRANEAN FLYING SAUCERS

Ray Palmer, who was a writer and editor of such magazines as *Amazing Stories*, *FATE*, *Search*, *Flying Saucers*, was often referred to as the 'man who created flying saucers.' With his background in science fiction, Palmer was one of the earliest publishers to realize that there was money to be made on the subject of UFOs.

Palmer first saw what a purportedly "strange-but-true" story could do for magazine sales when he first discovered Richard S. Shaver in 1943. Shaver had written to Palmer, who was editor of *Amazing Stories* magazine, with a weird tale of ancient extraterrestrial races, Atlantis, spaceships and bizarre creatures called Dero who lived in vast tunnels that criss-crossed beneath the surface of the planet.

After Palmer printed a re-worked version of Shavers story called *I Remember Lemuria*, Amazing Stories was flooded with letters from readers who purportedly had similar experiences with the subterranean world and the creatures that dwelt there. Palmer was keen to observe that the Shaver Mystery, as it would later be known, and people's positive, if not fervent, reaction to it, was strikingly similar to the UFO mystery that surfaced more than a decade later.

Because of his previous experiences with the Shaver Mystery, Palmer would never commit himself to the extraterrestrial explanation for UFOs that had become so predominant by the 1950s. Instead of looking to the heavens for flying saucers, Palmer looked downwards into the hollow Earth as a possible point of origin.

In the December, 1959 issue of *Flying Saucers Magazine*, Palmer wrote:

Admiral Byrd's Secret Journey Beyond the Poles

"In this issue we have presented the results of years of research, in which we advance the possibility that the flying saucers not only are from our own planet, and not from space, inner or outer, but there is a tremendous mass to evidence to show that there is an UNKNOWN location of vast dimensions which is, insofar as we can safely state at this writing, also unexplored, where the flying saucers can, and most probably do originate."

In reference to the claims made by some flying saucer contactees that they were taken up on a flying saucer for a trip to Mars and other planets, Palmer says:

"We've read all the accounts of such voyages and nowhere, in any of them, can we find positive evidence that space was traversed: In all these accounts, we can see where the passengers could have been taken to this 'unknown land' discovered by Admiral Byrd, and if told they were on Mars, they would not know the difference.

"Provided an actual trip in a saucer was made, the pilots of the flying saucers could have simulated a space trip and instead took their passengers to 'that mysterious land beyond the Pole,' as Admiral Byrd calls it."

In an article *Saucers From Earth: A Challenge to Secrecy*, in the December, 1959 issue of *Flying Saucers*, Palmer wrote:

"*Flying Saucers* magazine has amassed a large file of evidence which its editors consider unassailable, to prove that the flying saucers are native to the planet Earth: that the governments of more than one nation know this to be a fact; that a concerted effort is being made to learn all about them, and to explore their native land; that the facts already known are considered so important that they are the world's top secret; that the danger is so great that to offer public proof is to risk widespread panic; that public knowledge would bring public demand for action, which would topple governments both helpless and unwilling to comply; that the inherent nature of the flying saucers and their origination area is completely disruptive to political and economic status-quo. Flying saucers have been with humanity for centuries, if not thousands of years. Their antiquity eliminates contemporary earth governments as the originators of the mysterious phenomenon."

After disproving that flying saucers come from any existing nation, Palmer attacks the theory of their interplanetary origin, whose chief proponent is the American flying saucer expert, Keyhoe, also some contactees who claim some flying saucers come from Mars, others from Venus, etc. After showing that flying saucers do not come from any existing nation or from other planets, Palmer concludes that they come from the earth's hollow interior through the polar opening:

"In the opinion of the editors of *Flying Saucers*, this Polar origin of the flying saucers will now have to be factually disproved. Any denial must be accompanied with positive proof. *Flying Saucers* suggests that such proof cannot be provided. *Flying Saucers* takes the stand that all flying saucer groups should study the matter from the

Admiral Byrd's Secret Journey Beyond the Poles

hollow earth viewpoint, amass all confirmatory evidence available in the last two centuries, and search diligently for any contrary evidence. Now that we have tracked the flying saucers to the most logical origin (the one we have consistently insisted must exist because of the insurmountable obstacles of interstellar origin, which demands factors beyond our imagination), that the flying saucers come from our own Earth, it must be proved or disproved, one way or the other.

"Why? Because if the interior of the Earth is populated by a highly scientific and advanced race, we must make profitable contact with them; and if they are mighty in their science, which includes the science of war, we must not make enemies of them; and if it is the intent of our governments to regard the interior of the Earth as 'virgin territory,' and comparable to the 'Indian Territory' of North America when the settlers came over to take it away from its rightful owners, it is right for the people to know that intent, and to express their desire in the matter.

"The flying saucer has become the most important single fact in history. The answers to the questions raised in this article are to be answered. Admiral Byrd has discovered a new and mysterious land, the 'center of the great unknown,' and the most important discovery of all time. We have it from his own lips, from a man whose integrity has always been unimpeachable, and whose mind was one of the most brilliant of modern times.

"Let those who wish to call him a liar step forward and prove their claim: Flying saucers come from this Earth."

According to Dr. Raymond Bernard in his book *The Hollow Earth*, Palmers editorial created a sensation and caused certain government secret agencies to confiscate the magazine and stop its distribution, so that it did not reach their over 5000 subscribers. Bernard declares that obviously the U.S. government was convinced that such an unclaimed, unknown territory, vast in extent, larger than the entire land surface of the earth, exists and wished its existence to be kept secret, so that no other nation would know about it or reach it before and claim this territory as its own. It was important that the Russians do not learn about it. For this reason it was decided to suppress this issue of *Flying Saucers* of December, 1959, which was mysteriously removed from circulation.

Evidently the information that flying saucers originate from the Earth's hollow interior through the polar openings, just like news concerning Admiral Byrd's flights past the Poles into the new unknown territory beyond them, was considered too dangerous to be released to the public and was consequently suppressed by government authorities.

Another flying saucer researcher at the time, Gray Barker, agreed with Palmer and put his own spin on the theory with his book *They Knew Too Much About Flying Saucers*. In it, Barker speaks of the "Antarctic Mystery" or the unusual number of

Admiral Byrd's Secret Journey Beyond the Poles

flying saucers seen to ascend and descend in the region of the South Pole, which strongly supports the theory of a polar opening through which flying saucers emerge from and enter the hollow interior of the earth.

In this book he mentions an Australian and New Zealand investigator, named Bender and Jarrold respectively, who believed that flying saucers originate and are based in the Antarctic and tried to trace their course, when they were suddenly stopped in their research by "three men in black," who were secret government agents who apparently wished to suppress such research, just as publicity concerning Admiral Byrd's 2,300 mile flight to the new unknown territory not found on any map, that lies beyond the South Pole and inside the opening that leads to the earth's hollow interior, was suppressed in the press.

Theodore Fitch was another writer who believed that UFOs originate from the hollow Earth. In his book, *Our Paradise Inside the Earth*, he writes:

"Writers of books on flying saucers believe that they come from other planets. But how can that be? They are too far away. Traveling at terrific speeds it would take a lifetime to make the trip (especially from planets of other solar systems)."

Fitch says that the UFO occupants who come to us in flying saucers and who pose to be visitors from other planets, are really members of an advanced civilization in the hollow interior of the Earth, who have important reasons for keeping their true place of origin secret, for which reason they purposely foster the false belief that they come from other planets.

"They say that they come from other planets, but we doubt it. This is a white lie in order to prevent militaristic governments from learning that on the opposite side of the Earth's crust there exists an advanced civilization whose scientific attainments far surpass our own, which is reached by the polar openings. In this way they protect themselves from molestation or possible war between subterranean and surface races."

Fitch agrees with Palmer that flying saucers are not space ships piloted by spacemen. Rather they are vehicles for atmospheric travel which come from the hollow interior of the Earth in which they fly, connecting each part of the concave subterranean world with the other.

In the 1950s, UFO occupants were often reported as being small in statue, with dark skin and hair. Fitch believed that these beings belong to the same subterranean race from which the Eskimos descended. Fitch is in agreement with William Reed and Marshall B. Gardner that the ancestors of the Eskimos came from the hollow interior of the Earth through the polar opening. Describing these UFO occupants, Fitch says:

"Though smaller than we, they are stronger. Their grip is like a vice. One of them could quickly overpower a strong man. Their bodies are perfect in build. Both men and women dress neatly. Though not beautiful, they are nice looking. Not one of them looks to be over thirty years old. They say that they do not expect to ever die.

Admiral Byrd's Secret Journey Beyond the Poles

"It would take a book to record the conversation that has taken place with the saucermen and women. Their speech is quick, sharp and right to the point. They seem to be very, very intelligent. They talk freely and answer all questions, but they lie about things they do not want us to know (refusing to reveal their true subterranean origin and pretending to come from other planets, as Mars and Venus).

"Here are a few brief statements or claims made by the little men and women who live inside the earth. They boast about their superior mentality and knowledge, and that they excel us in creative ability. They say they are far ahead of us from the standpoint of new inventions.

"For instance, they claim that their flying saucers are powered with 'free energy' (meaning the electromagnetic energy of space, which is free and not like fuel used to supply our aircraft). They claim they obtain this 'free energy' by exploding certain atoms by the action of the electromagnetic energy of space while in flight.

"They say they are thousands of years ahead of us in all of the arts, such as painting, sculpture and architectural designing. In addition, they are ahead of us in their domestic and business management, in their agricultural techniques, and that their beautiful landscapes, parks, flower gardens, orchards and farms vastly surpass our own.

"They claim that they are far ahead of us in their knowledge of nutrition and diet. They claim to live in luxury, yet have no class distinction and no poverty among them, nor need of police. They say that they know every language on earth."

Fitch describes these people as living under an economic system where all material possessions are owned in common, without private aggrandizement or hoarding and without class distinctions of rich and poor, capitalist or worker. Also they have an equitable system of distribution free from exploitation and usury; and there is no poverty among them, since all are on a basis of perfect equality through a system of common ownership. They have no private property and work together cooperatively for their mutual welfare. Fitch writes:

"They say they know all the secrets of every government. They say they are of higher intelligence and authority. Since they are our superiors they have authority over us. They claim to be experts in mental telepathy. They claim they came from an antediluvian race (Lemurian and Atlantean). They say they know nothing at all about our Jesus, and say our Bible has been mistranslated, misinterpreted and misconstrued. They claim that they are a race which has not fallen as we have...They say we should get rid of nuclear bombs and armaments."

Earlier in this chapter, we referenced Dr. Raymond Bernard who is probably best known for his book ***The Hollow Earth***. Dr. Raymond Bernard was the pen name of Dr. Walter Siegmeister who spent many years searching South America for entrances to underground civilizations he believed existed beneath the surface. After the U.S. exploded the atomic bomb, Bernard became concerned about the planets rising

Admiral Byrd's Secret Journey Beyond the Poles

radiation levels, but believed South America would be a relatively safe haven should an atomic war develop.

Dr. Bernard settled in Joinville, Santa Caterina, Brazil, where he hoped to set up a colony for people throughout the world who wanted to come and develop the rich agricultural area and escape what he believed to be a coming atomic holocaust. Bernard was positive that UFOs came from the hollow Earth and used secret tunnels that were scattered all across central and South America to gain access to the surface world.

In 1964, Dr. Bernard claimed that he had found the entrances to several underground cities and had actually entered some of these portals to the inner Earth. He said that with the help of about twenty other explorers they had spotted the location of about fifty underground cities in Brazil that he suspected were the remnants of the destroyed land of Atlantis who had fled their homeland and later settled in Brazil.

One of Bernard's explorers relayed an amazing story that seemed to confirm his belief in the hollow Earth. Dr. Bernard referred to his friend as R.K. because of the incredible nature of his story; he did not want his identity revealed.

A certain hunter who had spent much of his life tramping through the mountains of Santa Caterina informed Dr. Raymond Bernard, director of our expedition, that one day he came across an immense tunnel inside of which he saw a giant air vehicle which he described as a zeppelin. Dr. Bernard therefore engaged this hunter to bring me to this tunnel. I entered the tunnel and found inside this strange immense air vehicle and its pilot, a subterranean man who was almost eight feet tall.

I wanted to take a photo of the air vehicle, but the pilot would not permit it. However he did invite me to ascend the staircase leading to a door in the vehicle, and I entered. It was magnificently furnished inside and could accommodate about forty passengers. The hunter who accompanied me also entered the vehicle.

I made a second trip to this same tunnel at a later date, this time alone. When I entered the vehicle, the door closed and I was taken for a trip. The vehicle had no windows and I was unable to see where I went, or perhaps the windows were purposely closed to guard certain important secrets.

There was no sound of any motor and the vehicle was completely silent. It was operated by a different form of energy, and so I concluded it was a giant cigar-shaped flying saucer. I expected it to leave the tunnel and fly in the sky, but instead it traveled deeper and deeper into the tunnel.

Then it began descending and I felt a strange sensation in my stomach, the same as when an elevator descends rapidly in one of New

113

Admiral Byrd's Secret Journey Beyond the Poles

York's skyscrapers. The descent took about half an hour and I figured the vehicle traveled at supersonic speed, because, as Dr. Bernard explained, showing me a diagram from his book, that what really happened was that the vehicle descended through an inclined tunnel connecting the Earth's surface with its hollow interior, perhaps the only such connection between the two worlds, excepting the north and south polar openings.

Finally, the feeling of descent in my stomach disappeared and it seemed that the vehicle was now flying horizontally. A large window at the bottom of the vehicle then opened, and much to my amazement I saw below me a large city.

This city was much different from the much small subterranean cities inside the earth's crust and not far from the surface, of which Dr. Bernard discovered more than sixty. These exist in Brazil, which was once an Atlantean colony and where Atlantis found refuge and constructed subterranean cities for protection against floodwaters." (NOTE: While these subterranean cities exist only in Brazil within the western World, it is probable that they also exist in the Far East...Dr. Bernard). The vehicle then made a curve in order to return, and as it did, it tilted, and much to my surprise I saw a sun in the sky, though smaller and nearer than our sun, and dimmer and reddish in color. This is the central sun described by Dr. Bernard in his books. It is a remnant of the original fire before the formation of our planet. The vehicle then began to ascend and finally it returned to its starting point.

I then returned to Dr. Bernard to tell him my experience. I really did not understand at all what I had gone through until he showed me diagrams from his book, *The Hollow Earth*, and explained that I was the first inhabitant of the Earth's surface ever to travel to the subterranean world in the hollow interior of the earth. He added that 1 made the greatest discovery and performed the greatest feat of exploration in history, much greater than that of Columbus, for while Columbus discovered a new continent, I discovered a NEW WORLD - THE SUBTERRANEAN WORLD.

I then told Dr. Bernard that I had forgotten to tell him one thing, namely that the subterranean pilot had told me that a great reception was being prepared for him in the center of the earth, when I will bring him there on my next trip, for as a leader of our expedition, the subterranean people will honor him as the first inhabitant of the earth's surface to establish communication between the Upper World and the Subterranean World.

Admiral Byrd's Secret Journey Beyond the Poles

This reception will take place in the City of Shamballah, world capital of the Subterranean World of Agharta. Here dwells the King of the World, its supreme potentate, ruling over millions of inhabitants of this empire. Dr. Barnard was thrilled when he heard of this invitation, for he has tirelessly searched and traveled for thirty-two years, covering more than twenty countries of Latin America to find what I found for him. He had spent the most of his personal fortune in his search for the inner earth empire.

THE MYSTERIOUS DISAPPEARANCE OF DR. BERNARD

This startling revelation was sent to Timothy Green Beckley who had been in correspondence with Dr. Bernard concerning a new book about the subterranean world. Bernard sent Beckley a request aimed at anyone interested in accompanying him to explore the inner world. This was the last that anyone ever heard from Dr. Bernard.

This is undoubtedly THE GREATEST FEAT OF EXPLORATION IN HISTORY. I wish all who want to help me to come here and let me bring them to the tunnel in which this vehicle is stationed.

There are certain basic requirements, however, before anyone can enter the Subterranean World. These were given to me by the leaders of that world. They are:

1. The applicant must abstain from all animal foods, and be a strict vegetarian, consuming no meat, fish, fowl, eggs, dairy products, honey, salt condiments, coffee, tea, cocoa, alcoholic beverages, etc.

2. He must not be addicted to the poisonous weed, tobacco.

3. Persons wishing to enter the inner earth must also be strictly chaste, for no sexual relations are allowed.

Right now there are about 100 individuals (men, women and children) in Santa Caterina ready to take up residence in the subterranean colony I am establishing, to be associated with one of the sixty subterranean cities I found, all of which have an abundance of fruits for the nutriment of their inhabitants. These fruits grow under the strange light that illuminates the subterranean cities. One such city was described by Bulwer Lytton in his book, *The Coming Race*.

The subterranean race of fruitarians, who live for centuries, will be the coming race after surface cities are destroyed by the lethal fallout of World War III. Belief in an impending destruction is widespread in Brazil and this compels many people to seek refuge in the subterranean world, to escape the deadly fallout caused by the coming war and the flood to follow. This flood will be caused by melting of the polar ice caps by the heated atmosphere caused by superbomb explosions.

Another one of my explorers discovered a subterranean city in which exist marvelous automata or mechanical robots. These robots perform all kinds of useful labor and have electronic brains which, strange to relate, possess a degree of intelligence of their own. They can speak, answer questions, talk, open and close doors, etc. These robots are controlled by radiations coming from a control dial, something like a typewriter, operated by a subterranean man.

When my explorer came to the door of this subterranean city, the robot opened the door and met him, together with the subterranean man who controlled him. The subterranean spoke Esperanto or a similar language, which had words from many of our languages, mixed together. When my explorer tried to take a photo of him, he grabbed the camera, which he later returned.

To enter the tunnel that leads to this subsurface city one must pass through poisonous gases and must wear a mask and carry a tank of oxygen. My explorer spent some time in the subterranean city of Atlantean scientists, operating strange devices. These subsurface world people ride in automatic cars that travel at supersonic speeds along rails or something like this. My explorer has been invited to bring eleven other people to this city and each newcomer can bring eleven more.

In this way, more and more people, who begin to realize that an inner earth really exists, can experience its actualities. They will also learn that the people who live in these cities are flesh and blood people who look, for the most part, just like you and me. Only their science and personal development is thousands of years more advanced than ours, on the outer surface of the planet.

It would be easy to dismiss this story as the ravings of a madman, or perhaps a scheme to steal money from the gullible. However, Timothy Beckley says that nothing could be further from the truth. Bernard's books were published by U.S. firms without royalty fees. He offered the tracts of land to be settled by colonists at very modest costs and offered to give land free to those who could not afford it.

It is evident that Dr. Bernard's source of income came from a relatively modest estate, inherited from his mother and amounting to about $100,000, upon which he lived and conducted his work during his years of searching for the inner Earth. Martin Gardner, who makes a living debunking the esoteric, claims that Dr. Bernard died of

Admiral Byrd's Secret Journey Beyond the Poles

pneumonia on September 10, 1965 while searching the tunnel openings in South America. However, Gardner offers no details on where he received his information concerning Dr. Bernard.

Since no records of his death have ever been found and considering his proposed trip into the inner Earth, it must be considered that Dr. Bernard either met with some accident in his explorations or actually penetrated the inner Earth, where he either met with an unfortunate fate, or is still living amongst the citizens of the underground world.

JOHN J. ROBINSON REPORTS ON UNDERGROUND ENTRANCES

The late John J. Robinson was a private researcher who, along with his charming wife, Mary, took a considerable interest in the hollow Earth, the Shaver Mystery, and UFOs. Mr. Robinson's many contributions to the major publications in the 1960s and 1970s, including Saucer News and Searchlight, brought in scores of letters from readers in response to his findings. Mr. Robinson has conducted extensive research about secret entrances to the inner world that he believes may exist in South America and elsewhere.

THE LIYOBAA CAVE ENTRANCES

After the conquest of South America by the Spanish Conquistadores, the Catholic priests who were attempting to convert the heathen Indians discovered a cave entrance to what they called "Hell." This entrance has since been sealed off with tons of rubble, dirt and huge stones and boulders.

The village of Liyobaa (or to translate it, "The Cavern of Death") was located in the province of Zapoteca, somewhere near the ancient village of Mictlan, or the "Village of the Underworld."

The Cavern of Death was actually located in the last chamber of an eight-chamber building or temple. This temple had four rooms above the ground and four more important chambers built below the surface.

The high priests of the then-prevailing Indian religion conducted the ordinary ceremonies for the common man of Theozapotlan in the upper rooms. It was when they descended into the subsurface chambers that the secret and, to them, holy ceremonies, were conducted. The first underground room was the one which was reserved for any human sacrifice. Its walls were lined with the images of the representations of their various "Gods."

A bloodstained stone altar in the center of the chamber served for the sacrifice of any human victim, whose still-beating heart would be torn from a screaming still-living body and offered to the lips of those same stone idols for their supposed repletion.

Admiral Byrd's Secret Journey Beyond the Poles

There was a second door in this first chamber which led to the second room. This was a crypt where the preserved bodies of all the deceased high priests reposed. The next door in this crypt led to the third underground vault, about the walls of which were the preserved bodies of all the former "Kings" of Theozapotlan. For, on the death of a king, his body was brought to this chamber and installed there with all the state and glory, as well as with many sacrifices to accompany him. It was from this burial chamber of kings that the fourth and last underground room was accessible. A doorway in this third room led into the last underground chamber which seems appropriately to have contained nothing but another entrance covered by a huge stone slab. I write "appropriately," for the entrance to either HELL or the CAVES should be covered but unencumbered in the area about it for the benefit of those who might wish to leave rapidly and wisely. It was conceived by the Catholic Fathers of that day that this was an entrance to Hades; however, as we may well understand, it was an entrance to a Dero larder.

Through this doorway behind the stone slab were placed the bodies of all human sacrifices as well as the bodies of all the great lords and chieftains of the land who fell in battle. The bodies of those warriors were brought from far and wide to be thrown into this cave when they had been cut down in the battles which were constantly being waged by these people.

Many of the common people, when debilitated by an incurable illness or oppressed by an unsupportable hardship, which made them seek death, would prevail upon the high priests to allow them to enter the door of death while still living. They believed that if they did so they would be the recipients of a very special afterlife.

The high priests would sometimes accept them as living sacrifices and after special ceremonies allow them to enter the "Cavern of Death" while still living. Needless to say, none ever returned to describe their experiences.

The Catholic priests, in order to convert the believers in this "myth" to Christianity, made arrangements to enter this subterranean door with a large retinue of torch holders and a long rope, which was tied to the stone slab door. They also took the precaution of having a large armed guard make sure that the door was not closed on them. After they had lighted their torches and entered the door, it was discovered that they would have to descend several very large steps.

At the foot of the steps was a very wide stone-paved passageway with a high stone buttress on either side. The passageway led directly away from the steps into the distant bowels of the earth. The bones of the most recent arrivals, picked clean, lay before them as the passage seemed to continue without end. On each side of the buttressed path they could see into a large open area which was a labyrinth of stone pillars that seemed to hold up the very mountains which they knew they were beneath. As they advanced into the mountain, a putrid, dank air assailed their nostrils, serpents retreated from the light of their torches and at times they seemed to see distorted figures retreat from the light behind the shadows of the pillars in the distance.

They continued into the depths a distance of about 40 meters when suddenly a strong cold wind began to blow about them. Still striving to continue, as their torches were extinguished rapidly, they took flight when all became dark, not only from the danger of the serpents, but also from strange sounds they could not place, but which were being made by the members of their own party. Using the rope and the light of the torch one of the guards held in the doorway, out of the strong wind, the entire party rapidly retreated from this terrifying region.

When all the company had swiftly retreated to the ante-chamber of "Hell," they rapidly replaced the large stone slab door. After this the head prelate gave orders to fill in all the underground chambers and seal off and erase all signs of the stairs to them, thus eradicating for all time this entrance to the Caves.

THE TUNNELS OF SOUTH AMERICA

In Southern and Central America, as well as in Mexico, the ancient people did not deny the existence of subterranean caves, chambers or tunnels. An examination of the religious beliefs of all these ancient civilizations will reveal this.

The Aztecs of Mexico had their dark, dreary and much-feared "Tlalxico" which was ruled by "Mictlan," their god of death. The Mayas of Yucatan held a belief in the existence of underworlds. These they termed "Mitlan," and they were icy cold as are most subterranean chambers or tunnels (for proof visit a large cavern in summer clothes and see how uncomfortable you are). These underworlds were presided over by "Ah Puch," the Lord of Death. We also have mention of the underground in the Mayan sacred writings, the "Popol Vuh"; as well as in the "Book of Chilam Balam of Chumayel." Even some of the codices seem to refer to them.

Peru and Chile, when they were ruled by the Incas, also reveal knowledge of the underground. "Supai," the god of death, had an underground dwelling, a much-feared "Place of Darkness." "Pachacamce," the god of the earth, caused underground rumbles in subterranean places where huge stones evidently fell, hours after he had shaken the earth with violence.

A legend of the first Inca "Manco Capac" relates that he and his followers, the founders of the Inca realm, came from underground caves, while the people of the time revered snakes because of "Urcaguay," the god of underground treasures. This god is depicted as a large snake whose tail has hanging pendent from it, the head of a deer and many little gold chains. Even the "Comentarios Reales de los Incas" of Garciliasso de la Vega hints at the existence of the subterranean.

Admiral Byrd's Secret Journey Beyond the Poles

References to the tunnels have come down to us from information that the Conquistadores obtained. From some unknown source they had gathered information that the wealth of the Inca's domain was stored in a vast underground runnel or a road, and Pizzaro held the Inca Atahuelpha prisoner in order to obtain his wealth, which, it was rumored, was stored in a vast subterranean tunnel that ran for many miles below the surface of the earth. The Inca, if he had the information regarding the entrance to this tunnel, never revealed it. The priests of the Sun God and the Inca's wife determined, it is asserted, the eventual fate of the Inca by occult means. The knowledge that Pizzaro did not intend to spare the Inca Atahuelpha's life caused them to seal up the entrance and hide it so well that it has never been found to this day.

A few Quicha Indians, who are pure descendants of the line of priests, are said to still have the knowledge of the location of the entrance to this tunnel. They are the appointed guardians of this escort, so it is rumored today in Peru.

Another source of tunnel information may be a huge monolith of perpendicular rock, which stands apart from its native habitat, the mountains. This rock is of lava, and how it was erected or who erected it is lost in the ages of antiquity, long before the Incas came on the scene. The huge monolith stands alone on the shore of Ila, a small town in the southern tip of Peru, not far from the Chilean border. The rock bears odd hieroglyphic marks carved upon it. Marks which only in the light of the setting sun create a cryptic group of symbols. It is said that these marks will reveal to the person able to read them and decipher the message correctly the location of a secret entrance to the tunnels, an entrance located, some researchers assert, in the fastness of the "Los Tres Picas," the Three Peaks region. This is a triangular formation of mountain tops near the monolith in the Loa River section.

When Mme. Blatvatsky visited Peru, she viewed and concurred with the information regarding the markings on the Ila monolith. She also asserted that information regarding the entrances to the tunnels had been graven in the walls of the "Sun Temple," at Cusco. Information of a symbolized nature, but nevertheless information which revealed to the person, with the knowledge of the meaning of the symbols, the secret entrances to those tunnels which the priests of the "Sun God" knew about. It is reported that Mme. Blavatsky received a chart of the tunnels, from an old Indian, when she visited Lima. This chart now reposes in the Adyar, India, archives of the Theosophical Society. Harold T. Wilkins, author of **Mysteries of Ancient South America**, also researched and inquired about the tunnels until he was able to conclude the following: Two underground roads leave the vicinity of Lima, Peru. One of these tunnels is a subterranean road to Cusco, almost 400 miles to the east. The other runs underground in a southern direction for more than 900 miles to the vicinity of Salar de Atacama. This is a large salt desert in Chile, the residue of the ocean water which was landlocked during an upheaval of the earth. The upheaval or cataclysm which created

Admiral Byrd's Secret Journey Beyond the Poles

Lake Titicaca raised Huanuco high above its place on the shore line. For information about this event, see the section titled "Tiahuanacu in the Andes" of Imanuel Velikovsky's Earth in Upheaval.

The Cordellerias domeyko, in that section of Chile, very evidently landlocked a great portion of the sea when it was raised. After the sea water evaporated, the vast salt waste, which is almost impossible to traverse, was left.

The tunnel, which has an entrance somewhere in the Los Tres Picos triangle, is also said to have a connection with this long southern underground road.

I conjecture that any continuation of the southern tunnel was broken during the cataclysm, which created the Andian mountain range. Such a continuation would have connected these ancient tunnels with the reputed Rainbow City center in the Antarctic.

I also conjecture that another event may have also happened during the shifting of the earth's crust at that time. Some of my readers may be familiar with the fact that at least one tribe of Indians in the Southwestern United States has a legend of coming from South America.

This legend relates a story of many years ago. The forefathers of the tribe are said to have lived in a large city far to the south. The story even ties the stars in the sky with the Southern Cross. The town may have been Huanaca before the earth shift which raised it above sea level. At any rate, the legend asserts that the people of this town in the south, the forefathers of a tribe of American Indians, were driven from their homes by a much more hostile and fierce group of warriors. The remnants of those who fled wandered for a long, long time in underground passages that led to the north. These passages eventually led them to our Southwest, where they emerged and set up tribal life once again.

How these ancient Indians were able to see in the dark does not seem to have been taken into consideration. The question of how these ancient tunnels of the Atlan or Titan were illuminated has long been of interest to those who follow the Shaver Mystery. It has long been considered that the tunnels were lit by a type of atomic light.

THE MALTESE CAVE ENTRANCE

The Maltese Cave entrance is on the island of Malta. This island is the largest of a group of three islands, in the sea that divides Europe from Africa, the Mediterranean. The little Maltese islands lay well off the coast of a much larger island, Sicily, halfway between the Libyan seaport of Tripoli and the Calabria of Italy's Calabrese people who are located in the toe of the boot like formation of Italy.

The three Maltese islands are composed of Gozo, Comino and Malta. They represent one of the smallest archipelagoes in the world, survivors of those remote days when continents were of a different shape. Those pre-cataclysm days when Atlantis and

121

Admiral Byrd's Secret Journey Beyond the Poles

Mu may have existed, the days when there was a land bridge between Europe and Africa. Those days when the entire Mediterranean area was merely a series of large lakes.

Malta is the principal island of the three. It reaches a width of almost nine miles, while it is all of 17 miles in length. Gozo is not as long as Malta is wide and Comino is almost a dot which separates them. Comino has at times boasted of a total population of 50 people. Malta is the most southern island, only 180 miles from the African coast. It was an ancient center of civilization at the time when the Phoenicians from Carthage invaded and began to rule it. At that time blood sacrifice was not new to the Maltese and they readily accepted the priests of Moloch as another name for "Baal," the Sun or Fire God. These priests offered up human sacrifices to their god, one who rejoiced in the sacrifice of human victims and the outcries of the victims' parents.

Since the time of the Carthaginians, Malta has had many rulers: Romans, Arabs, Normans, Aragonese, Castillians. Then France ruled the island for a short time before it became the British possession it now is.

However, with all this varied history, and regardless of the many nations who ruled them, the people of those islands still speak the ancient Canaanite, Semitic tongue, the speech of the Phoenicians, and the mother tongue of Queen Dido, who was the founder of Carthage. Malta was the birthplace of Carthage's most famous citizen, the man who made Rome tremble at the height of its power: Hannibal—one of the world's greatest generals.

On the northeast shore of Malta there are a number of large bays. One of these is known as Grand Harbor. This bay has a point of land extending into it upon which the capital of the Maltese Islands, the city of Valletta, is built. A few miles inland from this town toward the south, overlooking the plain which leads to the shore, is a large plateau known as the Corradino. The little village of Casal Paula is built on this plateau, and from the village one can view Valletta, Grand Harbor, the plain leading to it, and also look out to the sea.

In this small village of Casal Paula during the year 1902 workmen, who were digging a well, literally fell into the earth. They had once again uncovered the outer room of the Maltese Cave entrance. Since the well was to be dug for a house which was on the main street named "Hal Saflieni," and because this first cave was later discovered to be a complex of caves, three of which were a series of chambers excavated out of solid rock on three even lower levels for each chamber, this entrance is known as the "Hypogeum of Hal Saflieni." A hypogeum is the Latin name for an underground structure.

Later this series of underground rooms was discovered to have been located in the middle of an ancient neolithic village. From the construction of the entrance stones, it is now assumed that at certain times a human sacrifice was chained before the entrance. The entrance and the walls and ceilings of some of the passageways and rooms have been found to be decorated with red ocher primitive art designs, but when first

122

discovered the three caves were crammed with as many as 30,000 skeletons of men, women, and children. After all these bones were cleared out, the primitive murals were discovered.

They took the forms of diamond shapes, as well as oblated and elongated ovals, all of which were joined together with wavy lines and whirls. These decorations had been created solely from the application of red ocher, by the most primitive of methods.

Once past the entrance, a narrow passageway leads down into the first room. It is in this room, that the "Oracle" may be found. The Oracle is a hemispherical hole in the wall, a hole which is lower than the mouth of an ordinary-sized man. It is about two feet in diameter, and one can speak into it. A curved projection carved out of the back of the cave then acts as a sounding board. The voice is amplified and caused to resound throughout all the other caves. It creates an effect which must have frightened the primitives into sacrificing many of the members of their tribe to the being who spoke with the "Voice of A God."

If you continue down through narrow and low passageways, you come to another room. The center of this room has a circular stone altar with runnels on it, the use of which can only be guessed at. Carved in the walls of this room are many niches, the bases of which are like bunk beds. They have hollows scooped out for the heads and bodies, as well as the feet of four-foot-high individuals and some are even smaller.

Leading downward from this room is a small, narrow passageway, ending in another even larger underground room, which has narrow slit-like entrances into other small caves which surround it. One opening, however, is a window into another cave, the entrance to which is covered by a huge slab of stone. This window looks down into what was evidently a prison, but how beings only four feet tall were able to manipulate the huge stone slab must remain a mystery.

An opening in the wall opposite the entrance to this cave leads to a passage narrow and tortuous, the entrance to the real caves. This passage ends on a pathway which extends along the side of a vast cleft in the earth, a pathway along the edge of a veritable chasm, a pathway which leads ever downward to the long underground tunnels and series of caves which are reputed to allow one to traverse the entire length of the island and even further.

Legend has it that these passageways at one time connected with the underground crypts from which the Catacombs of Rome were created. This may very well be true; for the reader must remember that the Mediterranean Sea was created after neolithic times by earthquakes and the shifting of the earth's crust. Therefore, while the ancient tunnels may have existed, they might have been closed by cataclysms of this type, with the knowledge of them coming down to us only in legends.

Admiral Byrd's Secret Journey Beyond the Poles

The tunnels under the "Hypogeum" have been sealed off ever since a school teacher took 30 students into the caves and disappeared, guide and all. It was stated that the walls caved in on them.

Search parties were never able to locate any trace of these people. It has been asserted that for weeks the wailing and screaming of children was heard underground in different parts of the island, but no one could locate the source of the sound. If the walls caved in, why the cave-in could not be found and excavated to free the children remains a mystery.

How the children could live to scream for weeks later is another involved puzzle. At any rate, the underground entrance to the caves in Malta has been sealed off, and nobody is allowed to investigate the site.

THE RAINBOW CITY

When considering the possibility of the hollow Earth being the point of origin for some unidentified flying objects, one of the oldest modern versions of this theory is the story of the Rainbow City. After Ray Palmer published in *Amazing Stories* magazine the strange story of Richard Shaver and his subterranean creatures called Deros, readers flooded the magazines mailbox with weird stories of their own experiences with the inner world.

One of these letters came from William C. Hefferlin and so impressed Palmer that the September, 1946 issue of *Amazing* contained four short articles written by Hefferlin. Each article described an amazing new invention which had come to the author, in Palmer's words, "from Tibet by mental telepathy." For example, one invention was a "circle-winged airplane" that sounded like a cross between a conventional airplane and a flying saucer.

Palmer was suspicious of Hefferlin's claims, but he also knew a good story when he saw it. Palmer hinted that although there are many people who say they are recipients of unusual information from Tibet, they might be unfortunates misled by the telaug machines of the Dero.

Hefferlin replied in the next issue that full construction information' could not be placed in the hand's of the general public, considering the current state of the world. He also made the ambiguous statement that the articles were "but a brief schematic of the entertainment field pertaining to the Rainbow City."

Palmer was intrigued by Hefferlin's mention of the Rainbow City and wondered in an editorial if it "is the headquarters, a deserted city of Shavers Elder Race under the ice of the Antarctic, where all the gadgets mentioned and thousands more are perfectly preserved for thousands of years. Unfortunately, there was no follow up and the

Admiral Byrd's Secret Journey Beyond the Poles

Rainbow City vanished from the pages of *Amazing Stories* leaving readers to speculate if Hefferlin had been silenced.

A few years passed and in 1947 and 1948 the Borderland Sciences Research Foundation began issuing bits and pieces of a document called **The Hefferlin Manuscript** written by William and his wife Gladys from their home in Livingston, Montana. The pair disavowed any connection with their story and the Shaver Mystery and said that Ray Palmer deliberately distorted their statements for his own purpose.

"Here in **The Hefferlin Manuscript**, Gladys Hefferlin wrote, "those distortions would be corrected and the real story would be told."

In 1927, according to Gladys, the Hefferlins were a young, mystically-minded couple living in San Francisco and there they met and became friendly with a man known only as Emery who shared their interest in the esoteric. In 1935, after the couple had moved to Elwood, Indiana, they stayed in touch with Emery and through a series of letters, worked to try and establish a type of psychic connection that they called "Controlled Mental Communication."

Gladys Hefferlin acted as the mental link in Elwood, while Emery, who was a powerful psychic, sent and received messages in New York. "Our communication," Gladys wrote, "is as fast as ordinary, open conversation."

"Soon after the three of them had established to their satisfaction that the telepathic messages were being accurately received on both ends, Emery began disappearing on mysterious errands around the United States and the rest of the world. Every so often he would send a psychic message to the Hefferlins to let them know where he was, but the reasons for his travels remained a mystery.

At about the beginning of World War II, Emery revealed to them he had been "working under orders" from a community of Masters beneath Tibet. The Masters, using the circular aircraft that William had detailed earlier in *Amazing Stories*, were undertaking an expedition to Antarctica to search for the fabled Rainbow City.

Emery was assigned to the search, and he spent painstaking months flying over the Antarctic, looking for clues that none but the initiated could detect. He told the Hefferlins that due to the future devastation that WWII and future wars were going to bring to Earth, it was critical that Rainbow City be located and brought back to life in order for the cosmic plan to be fulfilled. On Thanksgiving of 1942, Emery sent a message to his friends; Rainbow City had been found.

As time went by, the Hefferlins learned more about Rainbow City and the concealed history of the human race. According to Emery, millions of years in the past, humanity ruled an empire of planets stretching over hundreds of galaxies. But at some point in their conquests, the ancient humans encountered the race which was to become their deadly enemy, the Snake People.

Admiral Byrd's Secret Journey Beyond the Poles

The Snake People and the ancients battled for a thousand years, with the advantage passing first to one side, then to the other. But it became clear that the Snake People had achieved the upper hand and they chased the human race from planet to planet, scattering the remnants of the human empire to a few lonely, inconsequential worlds.

One of these planets was Mars and home for hundreds of generations of the ancients. However, as time passed the ancients realized Mars was losing its water and oxygen.

The Great Ruler of Mars sent a fleet of spaceships to Earth where they settled in Antarctica and built seven great cities modeled after the cities on Mars. Each city had a distinctive color and was called the Green City or the Blue City or the Red City, but the greatest of all was Rainbow City, so named because it was constructed entirely of plastic of all colors of the rainbow.

Under their guidance of the Masters, the colony flourished under humanity's golden age. Unfortunately, a great catastrophe struck the earth and tipped it over on its axis, plunging Antarctica into its current icy and uninhabitable location. The survivors of the disaster abandoned the great cities to settle throughout the rest of the planet and after thousands of years of adversity they lost their technological knowledge.

Memories of the glorious days of the ancients became myths and legends. But even after all that time the great cities of the Antarctic still existed, buried now under thousands of feet of ice. Rainbow City sat deserted for a million years free of ice due to hot springs beneath the city.

Encircled by walls of ice ten thousand feet high, Rainbow City has remained hidden from Antarctic explorers to this day—except for Emery and his band. They occupied the city and found it consisted of six levels, one on the surface and five beneath it.

Since the technology of the ancients was infinitely superior to our own, the city was found with all its incredible machinery running as well as it had when the city was built two and a half million years ago. While preparing Rainbow City for resettlement by the Masters and their specially-selected followers, Emery and the others discovered many incredible devices abandoned by the ancients.

One of their most remarkable inventions was the "portal," a closet-like room with two doors that would warp space and deliver people or cargo to any point on the globe. The explorers also found and tested the ancients' enormous subway system that had hundreds of thousands of miles of tunnels from the central terminal beneath Rainbow City and snaking under all the continents and oceans.

Enormous trains a hundred feet in diameter had flown through the centers of the tubes, held in place by vibrational power; the cruising speed of the trains was over two thousand miles an hour. Emery's group explored a few of the nearby tunnels, and took one of the ancient trains on a short run beneath Antarctica, but the majority of the worldwide tube system was sitting unexplored and empty, as it had since the great disaster struck a million years ago.

Emery located a few of the great sub-terminals of the system under Asia, Africa, and the Americas using the portals and found them filled with unused atomic weapons, mostly personal "blaster types." The Hefferlins themselves discovered the end of one of the subterranean branch lines some two hundred feet or more up the side of a mountain west of Sheridan, Wyoming. "This tunnel seems to have been twisted and sheared off," William wrote. "We shall use the portals to find out what happened to them."

With the successful discovery of the Rainbow City, the Masters decided to send squadrons of circle-winged planes into the skies of every continent to search for more traces of ancient cities that might be revived; when people saw the strange craft, they mistook them for alien spaceships and called them flying saucers.

The Hefferlins faded into obscurity in the early 1950s, but the Rainbow City was not forgotten. In 1960, writer Michael X published a book titled ***Rainbow City and the Inner Earth People***. Michael X revealed that at the time of the pole shift, many of the ancients had fled into the hollow Earth where they built great cities much like the ones they had abandoned on the surface.

When the Masters on the surface rediscovered the Rainbow City, a special beacon was activated in the underground cities. The inner Earth residents knew that only those of a highly spiritual nature could find the Rainbow City, so using their disc-shaped aircraft, they began expeditions to the surface world to find their spiritual brethren.

With the help of the Guardians, a race of extraterrestrials from the hollow interior of planet Venus, the Masters are slowly removing the Dero and other destructive beings from the planet. "Both the astral and physical levels of the inner Earth," Michael X wrote, "are being cleaned out in preparation for the coming Golden Age."

The Masters and Guardians use Rainbow City as their way-station when passing in and out of the south polar opening which is around 2400 miles from the South Pole. According to Michael X, Rainbow City and the north and south polar openings are not easy to locate because they are camouflaged by the inner Earth people using advanced technology. This is why only the most spiritually enlightened has ever been able to visit these hidden locations.

THE GREEN CHILDREN OF WULFPETERS

If there is a world beneath our feet, and various races of people do live in the underworld, it is only reasonable that they should emerge upon occasion. The most famous case involved the discovery of two subsurface children in the year 1100, in the

Admiral Byrd's Secret Journey Beyond the Poles

small English town of Wulfpeters. The entire story is related in Chronicon Anglicarum, by Abbot Ralph, of the nearby community of Coggeshall. We quote this text as follows:

"This boy and girl, brother and sister, came out of holes at Mt. Mary de Wulfpeters, next to the edge of a pit found there. They had all the members, like those of other men; but in the color of the skin they differed from all other mortals of earth. For the surface of their skin none could understand. At that time, weeping inconsolably, they were taken, out of astonishment, to the house of Richard de Calne at Wikes.

"Bread and other food was placed before them; but they would not eat, and indeed, with great hunger from fasting, they were a long time tormented, because, as the girl afterwards confessed, that all that food could not be consumed by them. However, at last, beans cut off or torn from stalks, were brought to the house and they fell on them with great avidity. So now those beans were given to them and they broke open the beanstalks, not the pod or shell of the beans, evidently supposing that the beans were contained in the hollows of the stalks. But not finding beans within the stalks they again began to weep, which, when the bystanders noticed, they opened the shells and showed them the beans themselves. Whereupon, with great joyfulness, they ate beans for a long time, entirely, and would touch no other food.

"The boy, however, grew weaker and weaker, and died in a short period of time. The girl, indeed, always enjoying good food and growing accustomed to whatever food one was pleased to set before her, completely lost the green color of her skin and by degrees regained the normal redblooded condition of the body. And after being regenerated by the holy waters of baptism, for many years remained in the service of the soldier, aforesaid, as from the same soldier and his family we often heard.

"She showed herself very wanton and lascivious. Indeed asked frequently about the men of her own country, she affirmed that all who dwelt in her land, or had lived there, were colored green, and no sun was perceived there, but that a brightness or shining such as would happen after sunset was visible at all times. Asked in what manner she had come from the land with the boy, she replied that they were following sheep and arrived at a certain cavern. On entering it they heard a certain delectable sound of bells and, in trying to reach the sweet sound, they wandered for a very long time through the cavern until they came to its end. Thence, emerging, the excessive brightness of our sun and the unwonted, warm temperature of our air astonished and terrified them. For a long time they lay upon the edge of the cave. When overcome with disquietude, they wished to flee, but they could not in the least find the entrance to the cavern, until they were seized by the people of the countryside."

According to Fortean researcher Pippa Braybrook, bones of strange giant beings were uncovered in 1904 by J.C. Brown in the slopes of the Cascade Mountains. These Mountains run from Northern California to British Colombia, bypassing the Mt. Shasta

Admiral Byrd's Secret Journey Beyond the Poles

area, known for its many weird mysteries. The bones were uncovered in an ancient tunnel cut into solid rock, "lined with tempered copper and hung with shields and wall pieces made of gold." Other rooms deeper in the tunnel contained similar objects, some carved with drawings and hieroglyphics comparable with Churchward's Lemurian art.

We are told that Brown left this treasure go unclaimed for 30 years. In 1934 he attempted to recover these ancient works. Friends claim that when they last saw him he was ascending into this area with supplies enough to last him for a month. He was never seen again.

More recently, a married couple looking for rock paintings, in the Casa Diablo area just north of Bishop, California, came upon a circular hole in the ground about nine feet in diameter which exuded a sulphurous steam. A few feet from the surface, the shaft took a tangent course which looked easily accessible.

The plucky pair descended and found the oblique tunnel opened into a horizontal corridor whose dripping walls, though now encrusted with minerals, could have been carved only by human hands. The light of their flashlight was turned to a corner in which a delicate carved face was visible.

While they gazed at it water began flooding into the cave from unseen ducts and they heard a weird music which seemed to be coming from another world. When they emerged, the water made the tunnel entrance look like a pool on the desert floor. A perfect camouflage to hide a secret entrance by races living underground.

Admiral Byrd's Secret Journey Beyond the Poles

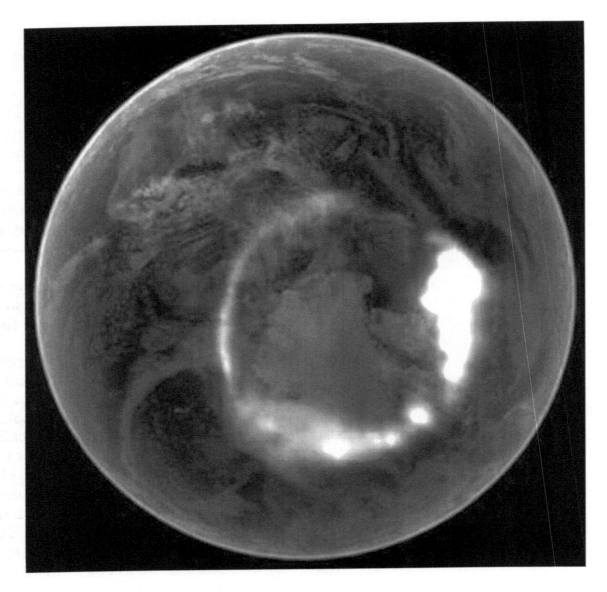

Satellite photo of aurora australis, or southern lights, shining through the southern polar opening.

CHAPTER ELEVEN
What Do the Bible and Other Holy Books Say About the Hollow Earth?

Myths and legends concerning the reality of the hollow Earth can be found in almost every civilization that has existed on the planet. With some careful study, references to the inner world are also found in holy texts that would eventually become the Torah, the Bible and the Qur'ān.

Brinsley le Poer Trench, the Earl of Clancarty said: "The Bible, as well as many ancient texts and manuscripts, make reference to the 'Underworld' below as a real and genuine dwelling place. I am of the opinion that religions have failed regarding their teaching of a 'Hell' below – because a deep scrutiny of the texts tells more of a 'paradise' rather than a burning abyss."

In the Hebrew Scripture, the Torah (the Five Books of Moses) and the Oral Tradition given at Mount Sinai, and within the mystical or metaphysical tradition known as Kabbalah, there are numerous references to worlds other than our own with life on them, both corporeal and incorporeal.

In the Hebrew language, every single word usually has more than one meaning. Every single letter – and even the size and various parts of an individual letter – contains additional information of profound consequence that may not only add to its definition an unfolding story, but may also provide essential keys to hidden Kabbalistic interpretations allied with the separate Oral Tradition that was handed down verbally by Moses to the Jewish People. For the scholar, none of this is too surprising, as it is known that everything that has happened, is happening, and will happen, is somewhere, at some level, encoded in a "divine formula" within the holy texts. This refers to not only generalities but to all the particulars of every single species and every single human being, including everything that will transpire in his or her lifetime, from the day of birth until the day of death, as well as all of his reincarnations and all of their particulars and minute details. This is true as well for every type of animal, plant and mineral.

Alongside the written Torah, the Oral Tradition is considered equally valid. Indeed, the exceedingly complex and comprehensive Talmud can be claimed to deal with almost any given topic in our physical and metaphysical universe. This is why in centuries past and even today, major scholars and mystics have been able to provide answers to riddles that even scientists have been unable to solve.

In the Book Judges (5:20), within the lines of the song sung by the Hebrew Judge, Deborah and Baraq son of Avino'am – on the day Yael drove a tent peg through the head

Admiral Byrd's Secret Journey Beyond the Poles

of the wicked King Sisera – there are a couple of highly intriguing verses with other worldly connotations. The first of these strange quotations reads: "They fought from heaven; the stars in their courses fought against Sisera," and the second (5:23), "Curse Meroz, said the angel of the Lord, curse bitterly its inhabitants; because they did not come to the help of the Lord against the mighty men."

But what does this 'Meroz' reference really allude to? In his book *Sefer HaBrit* (Book of the Covenant), Rabbi Pinchas Eliyahu Horowitz, (18th century) quotes as his authority a clear Talmud reference when he contends that Meroz is an inhabited planet somewhere in outer space. Furthermore, he states emphatically that God created an infinite number of worlds, of physical, spiritual and inter-dimensional nature.

This view is upheld by the Ari'zal (Rabbi Yitzchak Luria), who also spoke of an "infinite number of spiritual worlds." All of this might even be taken to indicate that the preceding battle described in Judges may even have extended beyond the boundaries of our planet's surface. Rabbi Horowitz was of the opinion that many planets are inhabited and that just as sea creatures differ from land creatures, because of their different environments, so too will natives of other worlds differ from human beings.

As well as references to worlds in outer space, there are abundant references to a hollow Earth, with multi-layered worlds existing right beneath our feet. In fact, it's a case of "as above, so below" echoing the Kabbalistic "unified theory of knowledge."

Just as there are said to be "seven Heavens," so too is it recorded that there are seven nether worlds, one above the other, each inhabited by its own species; one notable source, the 17th century Kabbalistic classic, *Hesed L'Avraham* by Rabbi Avraham Azulai, tells us that there are as many as 365 different species of beings living under the Earth's surface.

The Zohar tells us, for one example, of an amazing encounter by Rabbi Hiya and Rabbi Yosi with one of the residents of an underground realm called Arka, who are human-like but have two heads. The two sages apparently stumbled upon this alien individual when he came up from an underground cave. The venerable Rabbis Hiya and Yosi actually conversed with him, the subject of what must have been a most intriguing conversation being the strange being's desire to know all about conditions in our surface world. Kabbalists believe that the underground worlds are also the domain of the so-called mazikim, the troublemakers or demons, and of a category of being known as the "fallen angels."

According to the Zohar, Adam, the original forefather of the human species, visited all of the subterranean worlds, and left progeny in each. It was not revealed as to who his female partners were. Moreover, one reference in the Zohar even places the Garden of Eden at the center of these underground worlds, without identifying which. Perhaps it was at the second level, known as Adamah, where Cain and Abel are said to have been born.

Admiral Byrd's Secret Journey Beyond the Poles

What is also apparent from a number of sources is that these underground worlds may not be quite as physical as is our own surface world. As well, the inhabitants may not possess material bodies quite like our own, but possibly a mix of physical and ethereal or astral.

In the sacred literature, Adam is said to have had a "body of light" before the Fall, prior to taking on a garment of skin, or more correctly, a fully physical body. Tradition also maintains that Adam was of immense stature before the fall and carried within his bodily cells all the souls of future humankind.

Gehinnom (Hell) is identified as being at the fourth level called Gey, while, at the fifth level, in a world called Nishiyah, there lives a race who are said to be short, androgynous, no noses and only two slits through which they breathe; a description that sounds surprisingly like the Grays that have dominated the modern UFO mythos. Furthermore, a translation of the word Nishiyah means something like "dreamlike" or "amnesiac." Earth, itself, is, of course, at the seventh level, and is known in the Zohar as Tevel.

DR. FRANK STRANGES

Dr. Frank E. Stranges is Founder and President of the National Investigations Committee on UFOs (NICUFO) and has lectured on the subjects of UFOs, space, science phenomena and the Bible throughout the world. He is considered to be a leading authority on UFOs and space phenomena. In addition, he is President of International Evangelical Crusades (a worldwide Christian Denomination) and International Theological Seminary of California.

Dr. Stranges was born in New York and educated in Brooklyn, Pennsylvania, Minnesota, and California. He holds degrees in Theology, Psychology and Criminology. He is probably best known for his contacts with Valiant Thor, a being from the planet Venus who met Dr. Stranges at the Pentagon in 1959.

When Dr. Stranges met his friend from the planet Venus for the first time in December, 1957, he was taken to a non-descript room in the Pentagon where he was greeted by a man who was about six feet tall, perhaps 185 pounds, brown wavy hair and brown eyes. His complexion appeared normal and slightly tanned. With a warm smile he extended his hand and greeted Stranges by name; "Hello, Frank. How are you?"

As Dr. Stranges gripped his hand, he was somewhat surprised to feel the soft texture of his skin, "like that of a baby but with the strength of a man that silently testified to his power and intensity." He also noticed that Valiant Thor had no fingerprints and was told that all Earth people were thusly marked since the fall of Adam in the Garden of Eden, during the very dawn of civilization as we know it today.

Admiral Byrd's Secret Journey Beyond the Poles

This was the beginning of a long friendship between the man from Earth and the man from Venus that continues to this very day. Dr. Stranges has met with Valiant Thor many times since 1957 and has been given some amazing information for his fellow inhabitants of this planet; that is for those who are willing to listen.

Valiant Thor has told Dr. Stranges that there is life on many other planets of which people on Earth know nothing.

"There are more solar systems for which man has not even given God credit," he said. "There are many beings that have never transgressed the perfect laws of God. Man does not possess the right to condemn the whole of God's creation because he himself has broken the perfect laws of God through disobedience."

At one point Dr. Stranges asked Valiant Thor about the inhospitable conditions on the surface of Venus, noting that scientists have determined that the surface temperature reaches in excess of 800 degrees Fahrenheit. Valiant Thor said that this was correct, but that the inhabitants of Venus actually live in the hollow interior of Venus, coming and going through openings at the North and South Poles; just as has been described in legends about the hollow Earth.

This statement amazed Dr. Stranges, who had never heard of such a thing as hollow planets. Because of this, he began research on his own and discovered a number of Biblical passages that seemed to confirm that the Earth, and other planets in the universe, is hollow, with conditions inside that are generally favorable to life, even when the surface is hostile.

For example, the apocryphal Book of Enoch, which predates the New Testament and was excluded from the Bible at the Council of Nicaea in 325 CE, is a treasure house of knowledge and wisdom concerning the hollow Earth. The Book of Enoch describes a number of cavities, valleys, or hollows in the Earth's shell where imprisoned are fallen spirits or angels and other sick or monstrous entities that are reserved for judgment once the divine plan for humanity is accomplished.

Nearby are other valleys or chasms containing the spirits of all those who have been victimized by these fallen entities, continually crying out for revenge. There are also areas reserved for those who have yet to die and be judged. Apparently, provisions have been made within the shell and astral regions of the planet for the temporal or permanent housing of all manner of souls or spirits.

Enoch speaks of proceeding to "the middle of the Earth," where he beheld a blessed land that is happy and fertile (25:1, 26:1). An angel shows him "the first and last secrets in heaven above, and in the depths of the Earth: In the extremities of heaven, and in the foundations of it, and in the receptacle of the winds" (59:2-3).

There are said to be cavities in the earth and 'mighty waters' under it (65:1, 87:5, 95:2). Enoch sees an abyss "opened in the midst of the Earth, which was full of fire" (89:34); the abyss is said to be "on the right side of the Earth," which has been

Admiral Byrd's Secret Journey Beyond the Poles

interpreted as meaning the north. There is also a reference to seven great rivers, four of which "take their course in the cavity of the north" (76:6-7).

In Psalm 48:2 of the Bible, Mount Zion is said to be "in the far north," and in Ezekiel (28:13-14) Eden, "the garden of God," is placed on the "holy mountain of God." In Hebrew tradition, the primeval Eden is sometimes said to be at the "centre of the Earth."

Many parts of the Bible were undoubtedly influenced by the pagan cultures that surrounded the Holy land. In the Greek writings *Critias*, Plato says that the "holy habitation of Zeus is situated in the centre of the world." In *The Republic*, he says that Apollo, the traditional interpreter of religious matters, delivers his interpretation "from his seat at the earth's centre." He also writes: "Apollo's real home is among the Hyperboreans, in a land of perpetual life, where mythology tells us two doves flying from the two opposite ends of the world met in this fair region, the home of Apollo. Indeed, according to *Hecataeus*, Leto, the mother of Apollo, was born on an island in the Arctic Ocean far beyond the North Wind."

In the *Phaedo* Plato speaks of many cavities and "wonderful regions in the earth, and of subterranean flows of water, mud, and fire." One of the cavities in the earth is not only larger than the rest, but pierces right through from one side to the other. It is of this that Homer speaks when he says "Far, far away, there lies Earth's deepest chasm called Tartarus."

In the Greek view, the lands of the living were divided from Tartarus, the land of the dead, by fierce obstacles, rivers, and bodies of water or fire. The greatest of these was Oceanus, which not only comprised all the seas of the world, but was also the largest of the rivers which the Greeks believed swept into and through Tartarus, to emerge from the underworld on the opposite side of the Earth.

Other subterranean torrents included Lethe, the river of forgetfulness, and the Styx, the river of death. Tartarus was said to sink twice as far below the earth as the earth was beneath the sky and to be bounded by many perils. As well as being the home of the dethroned gods called the Titans, it contained a variety of regions or kingdoms, ranging from the Elysian Fields to the many grottoes, caverns, and pits of torment reserved for the damned. In the Sumerian epic of *Gilgamesh*, the underworld or "Great Below" was a place of immense size and great terror, filled with a wide range of beings, including spirits, the undead, humanoids, and savage guardians. In his search for everlasting life, Gilgamesh first had to reach the mountain of Mashu, connected with the heavens above and the netherworld below.

Having been allowed to enter the gate, he descended into the bowels of the Earth through twelve double-hours of darkness before reaching "an enclosure as of the gods," filled with brilliance, where there was a garden made entirely of precious stones.

135

Admiral Byrd's Secret Journey Beyond the Poles

According to Diodorus Siculus, the Chaldees imagined the Earth to have the form of a round boat turned upside down and to be hollow underneath.

The Bible describes the underworld or hell as a "bottomless pit" (Revelation 9:1-2) and "the abyss" (Romans 10:7), a place of punishment and misery, the abode of Satan and his demons. Other references to subterranean realms and life include the following:

. . . at the name of Jesus every knee should bow, in heaven and on earth and under the Earth . . . (Philippians 2:10, Revised Standard Version)

And no one in heaven or on Earth or under the Earth was able to open the scroll or look into it . . . (Revelation 5:3)

And every creature which is in heaven, and on the earth, and under the earth, and such as are in the sea . . . (Revelation 5:13)

In saying, 'He [Christ] ascended,' what does it mean but that he had also descended into the lower parts of the Earth? (Ephesians 4:9)

For as Jonah was three days and three nights in the belly of the whale, so will the son of man be three days and three nights in the heart of the Earth. (Matthew 12:40)

He stretches out the north over the void, and hangs the Earth upon nothing. (Job 26:7).

There was a certain rich man, which was clothed in fine linen, and fared sumptuously every day: And there was a certain beggar named Lazarus, which was laid at his gate, full of sores, And desiring to be fed with the crumbs which fell from the rich man's table: moreover the dogs came and licked his sores. And it came to pass that he died, and was carried by the angels into Abraham's bosom: the rich man also died, and was buried; And in hell he lift up his eyes, being in torments, and saw Abraham afar off, and Lazarus in his bosom. And he cried and said, Father Abraham, have mercy on me, and send Lazarus, that he may dip the tip of his finger in water, and cool my tongue; for I am tormented in this flame. But Abraham said, Son, remember that you in your lifetime received your good things, and likewise Lazarus evil things: but now he is comforted, and you are tormented... And beside all this, between us and you there is a great gulf fixed: so that they which would pass from here to you cannot; neither can they pass to us that would come from there . . . (Luke 16:19-26)

In the New Testament, in between the time Jesus dies on the cross and before the resurrection, he journeys to a strange land below the Earth. The New Testament understanding is that before the death and resurrection of Jesus, all who died in faith could not leave this inner world until a way back had been accomplished.

After the death and resurrection of Jesus, he descended to declare a further judgment upon the angels that sinned in Taratus and set the captives free in paradise.

Admiral Byrd's Secret Journey Beyond the Poles

In Matthew 27: 52-53 it says: *...and the graves were opened and many bodies of the saints which slept arose. And came out of the graves after his resurrection and went into the holy city and appeared unto many.*

After this time the upper half of Sheol was left empty. Now, upon death of those born of the Spirit they go directly to be with the Lord in the heavenly dimension. (2 Corinthians 5:8)

There are even parts of the Bible that seem to suggest the existence of the North and South polar openings. Dr. Stranges says that he discussed this with several universities and they him in private that they are beginning to do some private investigations into the theory, especially since they saw the NASA pictures that Stranges has that show a distinct opening at the South Pole. The United States Government with satellites have detected certain openings in and around the poles as well as in Alaska and many other places of which they have no rational explanation.

Dr. Stranges has three satellite photographs that show the South Pole; the first photo shows the South Pole clouded over. The second time around, 50% of the cloud covering was gone. And the third time around, there was an opening at the pole that has been estimated as being approximately 1500 miles across.

The Bible, according to Dr. Stranges, does speak of polar openings. *The waters are hid as with a stone, and the face of the deep is frozen.* (Job 38:30)

The waters "hid" are the internal waters of the deep or abyss. Like a stone on top, the excess floodwaters that are now frozen cover the face or opening of the abyss. This ice covering is what we call the Arctic and Antarctic circles. Frozen like a rock to cover the openings of the inner earth and the waters "hid" within.

He gathered the waters of the sea together as an heap: he layeth up the depth in storehouses. (Psalms 33:7).

He hath compassed the waters with bounds until the day and night come to an end. (Job 26:10)

He hath compassed literally means a circle of ice has been inscribed over the face of the waters. Before the Biblical flood, there was easy access in and out of the polar openings. This could explain why the holes are difficult to find, they are covered in ice and clouds.

For this they are willingly ignorant of, that by the Word of God the heavens were of old, and the earth standing out of the water and in the water: Whereby the world that then was, being overflowed with water perished: But the heavens and the earth, which are now, by the same word are kept in store, reserved unto fire against the day of judgment and perdition of ungodly men. (2 Peter 3:5-7)

The Greek word for Earth means in general term, arable land. The Greek word, sunistao, for standing is better rendered, united together. In this sense submerged land

Admiral Byrd's Secret Journey Beyond the Poles

or flooded land is not what is mentioned here but rather surface land out of the waters, and surface land in the waters (subterranean).

With this understanding we can see that the arable land was united together out of the water and in the water. But the flood changed this. Verse 6 states that the world (ordered arraignment) before was destroyed in the flood. Now the face or openings at the poles are covered over by the frozen floodwaters and the inner and outer realms separated from each other.

The Bible seems to be saying the inner world is separated into two chambers. One chamber is empty of population, its opening sealed off until the end of time. The other chamber thrives with a population that may be the Fallen angels in Tartarus (a lower level in Hades) or departed souls of the damned (upper level of Hades) or east of Eden in the land of Nod; in other words, humans.

This lower chamber will be breached at sometime in our history. A possible rendering of Job 26:8 states: *He binds up the waters as a thicket (a fortress) before broken into a hidden opening underneath.*

Finally, Dr. Stranges says that there are still to this day many adversaries to human freedom. These parasites have imbedded themselves in all phases of human society and will never be exposed except by extraterrestrial intervention.

There are confused individuals who have perfected a saucer-type aircraft. Some of these are the result of an attempt by some to institute a master race. Remnants of this group still exist.

These craft which they designed are still seen from time to time in areas of South America where some of those involved in the original plans still reside. These should not be confused with the spacecraft originating from other worlds or those coming from the interior of this planet. Nor should the occupants of craft originating from other worlds be confused with those "evil messengers" who do not originate from Earth but were cast into it after the first "war" ever recorded. They are in league with Earthly low-grades who have condemned themselves because of their own choices.

As has been discussed in earlier chapters of this book, Dr. Stranges seems to be saying that UFOs are actually a number of different types of phenomena that superficially resemble each other. Some appear to be benevolent; while others operate with domination as their goal. It is no coincidence that Dr. Stranges specifies a group that wants to institute a Master Race and that their flying saucers now are operating out of South America.

This appears to confirm the theory that Admiral Byrd encountered a Nazi stronghold in Antarctica that was using highly advanced flying discs. After this discovery in 1947, the Nazi base shifted its operations to South America – where there have been rumors of an extensive network of ancient underground tunnels, some still being used by a mysterious race of inner Earth beings.

Admiral Byrd's Secret Journey Beyond the Poles

Those who embrace the extraterrestrial hypothesis of UFOs find it easy to scoff at the idea that remnants of Nazi Germany could still be operating out of secret locations in South America and even some sections of the inner Earth with the assistance of an underworld race of humanoids. Considering the ancient worldwide traditions that say the inner world exists and is populated by a rich variety of intelligent races, it is no more difficult to imagine that some UFOs could be from right here on planet Earth then it is to imagine them traveling thousands of light years from some far, distant planet.

So the next time someone says to "keep your eyes to the skies," perhaps you should also spend a little time looking downwards, for as above, so below.

Admiral Byrd's Secret Journey Beyond the Poles

A SPECIAL THANKS

I would like to thank the following people for their help in making this book possible.

Timothy Green Beckley - Author of such hollow Earth books as:
The Shaver Mystery and the Inner Earth; *Subterranean Worlds Inside Earth*

Dr. Wendy Lockwood Ph.D. - Web of Light
3150 John Wallace Rd. #102
Evergreen, CO 80439

Dennis Crenshaw - Editor of *The Hollow Earth Insider*
www.thehollowearthinsider.com

Dr. Brooks Agnew - Phoenix Science Foundation
www.phoenixsciencefoundation.org/APEX.htm

Branton – Author of: *Reality of the Serpent Race
And The Subterranean Origin of UFOs*
www.angelfire.com/space/branton/signature.html

Dr. Frank Stranges – Author of: *Stranger at the Pentagon*
National Investigations Committee on Unidentified Flying Objects (NICUFO)
21601 Devonshire St. #217
Chatsworth, CA 91311-8415
www.nicufo.org

Dennis Crenshaw – *The Hollow Earth Insider*
www.thehollowearthinsider.com

Admiral Byrd's Secret Journey Beyond the Poles

For more information about the hollow Earth and other incredible books, videos and audios, send your name and address for your FREE catalog and subscription to our FREE weekly online newsletter.

Global Communications
P.O. Box 753
New Brunswick, NJ 08903

www.conspiracyjournal.com

Admiral Byrd's Secret Journey Beyond the Poles

13154094R00080

Printed in Great Britain
by Amazon.co.uk, Ltd.,
Marston Gate.